Participation Nation

Reconnecting Citizens to the Public Realm

Involve, 212 High Holborn, London WC1V 7BF
020 7632 0120 info@involve.org.uk www.involve.org.uk

ISBN 978-0-9552421-4-4

2007

Contents

Acknowledgements

Involve and IIPS would like to thank all the authors who have contributed their time and ideas to make this publication possible.

Involve also thanks all the speakers of the four Participation Nation seminars that took place between March and May 2007, and Ben Page and Debbie Lee Chan at Ipsos MORI who generously contributed time and financial support to make the seminars happen. Personal thanks also got to Ali Howes, Edward Andersson and Alice Casey for this assistance with the seminars and this publication.

In addition we thank Susannah Wight who copyedited the book.

Disclaimer

About Involve

Involve is a not-for-profit organisation specialising in understanding public engagement in all its forms. The organisation was set up by a number of leading practitioners and researchers in the public participation field and is chaired by Geoff Mulgan.

Involve provides advice, training, research, events and networking services to organisations and individuals interested in public participation. The organisation focuses on the practical reality of public participation and has four core activities:

— **Advocacy** – building the case for genuine citizen empowerment
— **New Thinking** – improving understanding of what works in public engagement
— **Better Practice** – supporting institutions and citizens to engage effectively
— **Networking** – bringing people from the participation and empowerment field together.

Involve's work is supported by the Joseph Rowntree Charitable Trust.

About IIPS

The *Institute for Insight in the Public Services* (IIPS) develops and promotes citizen insight to support the transformation of public service delivery in the UK.

About the authors

Douglas Alexander MP is the Labour MP for Paisley & Renfrewshire South. He is currently the secretary of state for international development.

Alice Casey is a researcher for Involve.

Viki Cooke co-founded Opinion Leader. Viki has played a leading role in pioneering deliberative methods to help shape policy including citizens' juries, citizens' forums and citizens' summits.

Stella Creasy is head of research and development for Involve.

Karin Gavelin is a researcher for Involve.

Valerie Hannon is the director of strategy for the Innovation Unit, a not-for-profit organisation promoting innovation in children's services and the public sector.

Michelle Harrison is the chair of the Institute for Insight in the Public Services (IIPS) and a director at Henley Centre HeadlightVision and BMRB.

Véronique Jochum is a research officer at the National Council for Voluntary Organisations (NCVO). She leads the research team's work on social capital and active citizenship.

Nick Johnson is the former head of policy for the Commission for Racial Equality and is a leading writer and commentator on issues of integration, equality and identity.

Nicholas Jones was a BBC industrial and political correspondent for 30 years (1972–2002) and has written extensively on the relationship between politicians and the news media.

Tony Juniper is director of Friends of the Earth. He has been a leading figure in many of the main environmental campaigns of recent times.

Debbie Lee Chan is a research director within the Participation Unit at Ipsos MORI.

Kirsty McNeill sat on the coordination team of Make Poverty History. She is a Labour councillor and the parliamentary candidate for Bermondsey and Old Southwark.

Ben Page is chairman of Ipsos MORI Social Research Institute, and managing director of Ipsos MORI Public Affairs.

Sophia Parker is an adviser on person-centred innovation and co-production to a range of organisations. She is also an associate at the think tank Demos.

Greg Power is a director of Global Partners and Associates. He was previously a special adviser to Rt Hon Robin Cook MP and Rt Hon Peter Hain MP.

Dave Prentis is the general secretary of UNISON. He is president of Unity Trust Bank.

Michelle Singer is head of knowledge venturing at Henley Centre HeadlightVision.

Laurie Waller is a researcher for Involve.

Karl Wilding is head of research at NCVO, where he directs a research programme around issues including the size, scope and value of voluntary and community organisations.

Susan Williams is leader of Trafford Council and has been a serving councillor for nine years.

Richard Wilson is director of Involve.

Foreword

By Rt Hon Hazel Blears MP

These are exciting times for those of us who are committed to community empowerment. As a nation we are currently renegotiating what it means to be a good citizen in the 21st century. The topic of this pamphlet could not have been more timely.

Policy making and politics is about finding shared solutions to the shared problems our nation faces. And whether obesity, climate change or terrorism, there are no shortage of issues to be addressed in the modern world. Yet I believe we can also find solutions to these problems by tapping the vast reserve of passion, knowledge and wisdom that resides in the British population.

So over the past ten years this government has sought to forge a new relationship between citizens and the state. From the national level – as set out in the Governance of Britain green paper – to the arena of local community – as outlined in the recent Empowerment Plan – we have devised wide ranging changes which bring decisions and power closer to citizens and the elected officials who represent them.

The arguments for and against community empowerment have bounced back and forth over the past years. My firm conviction is that the time for talk is over. I have a fundamental belief in the ability of people to work together – a belief grounded in my experience as Secretary of State, as an MP and as a citizen. I got involved in politics because of my belief in the power of local activism, in local decision making and action to achieve change. People are not the problem, they are the solution.

Yet for this to be the case we need to take concrete steps to ensure that our diverse communities are empowered to make a difference. The passing of the Local

Government and Public Involvement in Health bill means real change – a real transfer of power towards both elected representatives and communities directly. Communities and Local Government has allocated £35 million in an action plan over 3 years. But government cannot change the relationship between citizens and the state on our own. We need everyone – from voluntary and community groups to businesses and citizens- to play their part.

So in the years ahead we need to step up to the plate when it comes to participation and empowerment. From community asset transfers to participatory budgeting, local communities now have control over real money, real assets and real power – but we can do more, much more.

The authors in this book celebrate the potential of participation across Britain – looking at how it has been used to improve policies and peoples' lives to inspire us to even further heights. In the varied contributions they show how and why we need to think big and act bigger. That is why I have set us the goal to see participation in the budgeting process across all local authorities in England within 5 years.

We need to transform this nation into a nation of citizens, a nation of activists – in short a Participation Nation.

The Rt Hon Hazel Blears MP
Secretary of State for Communities and Local Government

Introduction:
Participation at the Core

By Stella Creasy

> Democracy is a device that ensures we shall be governed no
> better than we deserve.
>
> George Bernard Shaw

Whether through the calls for direct democracy, participatory budgeting, "double devolution" or choice and voice in service provision, never before has there been such a push to offer citizens so many time-intensive opportunities for direct influence over public services. In his first speech as prime minister to the British parliament, Gordon Brown stated:

> we will only meet the new challenges of security, of economic
> change, of communities under pressure – and forge a stronger
> shared national purpose – by building a new relationship between
> citizens and government that ensures that Government is a better
> servant of the people.[1]

These comments reflect how across the public realm there is a growing consensus that the state can no longer direct the actions of citizens without their cooperation any more than the market alone can be relied on to address the challenges of modern life. Whether in dealing with climate change, public health concerns or tackling international terrorism and promoting pro-social behaviour, we are entering an era in which progress can only be made in a society in which individuals, communities and public services are each able and willing to play their own part. For this to happen public participation must become the core, not the counterpart, of the future of public service decision making and delivery. The time has come for people power.

Yet if this rush to involve citizens makes sense to politicians and policy makers it holds little resonance outside Westminster. Among a public that exhibits a persistent and growing detachment from the traditional institutions of political engagement, there is little appetite for either new or old forums for democratic participation. Attitudinal evidence shows how ideals of social solidarity and the value of being a "good citizen" are seen as having little to do with taking part in politics or civic action.[2] So too, government is not the only body making a claim for the attention of people already struggling to balance the competing demands of work and family life. Whether marching in Whitehall, signing petitions in their town squares or buying wrist bands to "Make Poverty History", the British public is giving time and energy to social rather than political outlets for their opinions. And it is not just social or charitable concerns that appear better at holding the attention and interest of today's citizens. In the ferocious competition for citizen airtime, policy makers and politicians are losing out to the innovative opportunities being offered by companies and campaign groups engaging with customers and supporters in pursuit of brand loyalty and social influence.

Whether not voting, not attending public forums or simply not trusting their politicians to get on with the job, Britain's democracy falters under these twin pressures of public disengagement and competition for citizen airtime. Those who argue for process solutions alone to reconnect the public to policy making, be they constitutional changes or citizens' juries, fail to understand that these mean little to ordinary citizens who think in issues not institutions. This reflects how too often public participation is sought because it is seen to be a panacea to institutional concerns – whether in response to protests at policy direction, a method for challenging ways of working within the public sector or a lack of trust in politicians. Yet no process of participation will secure the support of every citizen for policies, no matter how well planned. Furthermore, to see the public only as a rubber stamping mechanism is to fail to value the contribution the public can make to policy outcomes in themselves. There is a danger in the current vogue for public engagement that confusion over methods and motivations on the part of both the public and politicians could quickly corrode the willingness of all to participate, much to the detriment of our democracy and society.

Done well, public participation can not only enrich our democracy by helping strengthen accountability for decision making, it can also encourage and empower our citizens to work with the state and each other to meet the challenges of our time. Debate and dialogue with the public can reveal new knowledge about how policy created in town halls and Whitehall is working out on the ground. That kind of intelligence is vital to making sure the intention behind policy becomes a reality. No strategy document can compensate for such real world information about what is making the difference and why. And in most cases both public and policy makers who engage in debate find the experience informative and relevant, as Involve's research[3] consistently reveals the value participants report they get from taking part.

Indeed, engagement can even speed the pace of progress by helping all parties to respond better to each other and create more responsive services. This in turn creates a momentum of responsibility which reaches far beyond questions of service provision. Whether encouraging people to get involved as members of a social campaign group, as users of services helping others by volunteering or by passing on information, being asked to participate can help spark and sustain activism. The interests, enthusiasm and commitment of citizens to a cause, their community or their country offer a vital resource with which to achieve outcomes. Engagement and empowerment activities can unleash this, building up "civic energy" within society by helping the public to learn the skills and confidence they need to be able to participate in either civil or civic action. The same can be said for those on the frontline as service providers whose professional knowledge and expertise can become a catalyst for shared successful outcomes for and with the public. Seen in this way, a nation in which citizens participate not only in decision making but also by actively contributing to its own future is one that can face the challenges of the modern era better.

How then to shift discussion about public engagement from a narrow concern for the legitimacy of decisions made to seeing citizen participation as the mode by which as a nation we unlock the potential of every citizen to get involved in shaping society? As a starting point, understanding the difference between consultation and empowerment can give clarity and direction to the unfolding debates on how, when and why to involve the public. Consultation should be about offering the public a genuine opportunity to comment and give feedback on public decision making. Recent events show that whether on healthcare, sustainable development or pension reform, citizen deliberation has informed and supported tough choices previously seen beyond the capacity of Whitehall to make.

However, too often good consultation with a commitment to follow through its outcomes in policy is the exception rather than the norm. So too the benefits of such involvement often only appear clear to those few hundred who actually take part in the consultation, rather than the majority of those affected by the outcomes. Deliberative methods can be used to deepen our democracy but they need to be matched by a commitment to delivering on their outcomes. Combating the growing cynicism about the value of deliberative methods will also require a commitment to resourcing methods that can help many more citizens and civil servants take part in such forums. We need to involve thousands, and perhaps even millions, in policy discussions in a manner that suits the lives of participants, not the institutional policy-making cycle.

If consultation is about good decision making, empowerment is about something other than how we offer better opportunities to comment on policy. It means building a participative culture in which all citizens feel able and willing to contribute, because this will bring benefits to society that are not available from state action or via the market alone. Agencies in the public realm should not fear the growth of social activism in British society but instead find ways and means of connecting and supporting it. Too often the manner in which public engagement forums are constructed asks citizens to choose between being active in their communities and participating in public debates, rather than asking how the state can collaborate and value this contribution to our social fabric. Furthermore, too often the people asked to participate are those who already contribute the most: the representatives of community groups or voluntary organisations who can find themselves in too many meetings and on too many committees to be able to engage in the grassroots work they enjoy. Conversely those who do not fit this mould or seek only to participate in an ad-hoc way can be overwhelmed and excluded because they don't understand the language or structures used and or feel they can live up to the expectations of the time they will commit.

If we want a participation nation then this needs to be constructed to reflect the lives of a wider range of people rather than the needs of policy makers alone. A timepoor public with families and social lives to cherish needs not only to be confident of the difference their contribution will make but also to be given practical help to participate. That both social and private sector organisations are at present winning the competition for citizen airtime by being more flexible and less structured in how they engage shows it is not only about the subject matter, but also how people are asked to be involved, which can make the difference to participation rates. The public sector can learn much from these sources about how to respond better to those who wish to be active occasionally or intermittently, as well as those prepared to go to meetings and commit their lives to helping in their community. Technology can also help facilitate easier participation, but if we are serious about being a participating nation then we must also act to make sure it is not only those who can dictate their own working hours or pay conditions who have the freedom to contribute. Supporting public engagement and social activism because of the benefits this offers society means there has to be legislation and leadership to ensure everyone has the time, money and opportunity not just to be with their family, but also to be active citizens.

Participation Nation: the pamphlet

It is against this backdrop that Involve has commissioned a variety of authors to look at what potential public engagement offers to our nation now and in the future. The first three authors reflect on how public engagement can make the difference between success and failure in three major policy challenges of the contemporary era. Taking three diverse concerns – social cohesion, educational attainment and climate change – Nick Johnson and Karin Gavelin, Valerie Hannon and Tony Juniper each show how engaging the public is not incidental but integral to making progress. Whether in seeking a nation which engenders solidarity among its citizens, empowers children to develop their own learning capacity or recognises the necessary changes in lifestyle that combating global warming will require, without seeking the public's commitment to these ambitions these authors all agree that little progress will be made.

Understanding the value that public engagement can offer policy making is only the start of making Britain a truly participative nation. Too often participation is offered in a format which makes sense to the institutions of governance. Challenging such an approach requires a better understanding of when and how engagement activities can be built into policy making and with what the public themselves will and will not engage. Getting the processes of participation right is the topic of concern to the next three authors, each speaking from a wealth of experience in working with a range of audiences. Viki Cooke from Opinion Leader Research (OLR) reflects on their experience of trying to secure support for decisions made by those not "in the room". Ben Page and Debbie Lee Chan from Ipsos MORI offer hard truths about when and if engagement is actually worthwhile. Finally Michelle Harrison and Michelle Singer from the Henley Centre look at the latest trends of where people are actually participating and what they do with their time when not engaged in public consultations.

Having looked at how participation might impact on policy directions and our democratic practices, the second section of this pamphlet looks at the response of differing key actors in the public realm. Turning first to the institutions of governance, Greg Power asks how, if parliament is serious in being the forum for public engagement, it must adapt to meet the challenges of the modern era. Complementing this, Cllr Susan Williams and Laurie Waller consider whether moves to devolve decision making to local authorities by the government will lead to a much needed revival in civic engagement. Yet recognising the value of citizen activism to society means looking beyond the traditional forums of the public realm to question who else is competing for the time and attention of the British public. As campaign organisations and volunteering become a part of everyday life, Kirsty McNeill from the Make Poverty History Campaign and Karl Wilding and Véronique

Jochum from the National Council for Voluntary Organisations (NCVO) ask what lessons the increasing social and civil activism holds for the public realm. After this, Nick Jones questions if the media can be a friend or foe of public engagement.

Finally, the third section of the pamphlet looks at what a participating nation means for those who traditionally have led on service delivery – public service providers, those working in public services and our political representatives themselves. Sophia Parker looks at the future of public services from the point of citizens, asking how they can become truly engaging so as to respond to today's self-acutalising individuals. Dave Prentis considers how public engagement can become not a contest between citizens and public service employees but a cooperative endeavour, then Douglas Alexander looks at how political parties can respond to the challenges that the changing British public realm presents. Lastly, Richard Wilson and Alice Casey from Involve consider the potential of new forms of technology and deliberative forums to increase participation in policy making. Complementing these perspectives is a short report back from the four "Participation Nation" seminars held between March and May 2007.

Each author comes to this debate from their own unique perspective, and indeed many would disagree with each other over the proposals they put forward. Yet each shares a concern to consider why and how public engagement will be at the core of the future of the British public realm. Thus, the range of discussion in this pamphlet reflects that there is no one solution to reconnecting British citizens to the public realm, but the benefits to democracy and social progress from such a reconnection are legion. In the months and years ahead in our research, practice and publications, Involve will seek to be at the forefront of challenging policy makers, press, politicians and the public about how and why we can truly become a participation nation.

> If liberty and equality, as is thought by some, are chiefly to be
> found in democracy, they will be best attained when all persons
> alike share in the government to the utmost.
>
> Aristotle

Notes

1. Gordon Brown, House of Commons statement on constitutional reform, *Hansard* 3 July 2007.

2. Henley Centre. 2007. *The Future of Citizenship*. London: Department for Constitutional Affairs (DCA).

3. Creasy, S., et al. 2007 *Engage for Change: The role of public engagement in climate change* policy. London: Involve; Gavelin, K. and Wilson, R. with Doubleday, R. 2007. *Democratic Technologies: final report of the Nanotechnology Engagement Group (NEG)*. London: Involve.

Part one: Participation in Action: Policy and Practice

All together now? Empowerment, engagement and cohesion

By Nick Johnson and Karin Gavelin

Our country is struggling to meet the demands of ensuring equality within diversity, and at the same time tackling the challenges posed by the threat of international terrorism, increased immigration, the rise of extremist groups and the changing dynamics of race and culture. In addition, Britain, like many countries across Europe, is grappling with the role that faith may play in the public sphere and how that is managed in a secular society. A way of navigating this territory is to see the challenges Britain faces beyond focusing solely on race and faith, providing policy makers with a different framework to tackle the pervasive inequalities and growing segregation in our society. This new framework should be founded on three key ingredients: *equality*, *interaction* and *participation*. First, to build strong and cohesive communities we need equality so people feel equally valued and empowered. We need interaction, so that people can develop relationships based on what they have in common, rather than being segregated by their apparent differences. The third, crucial, part of this agenda is ensuring there is full and meaningful participation, so that everyone can have a say and positively influence decisions and policies to meet their needs. All groups in society should expect to share in how we make decisions, and to carry the responsibilities of making society work.

The value of active participation to our wider civil society is clear. Full participation in making society work produces a range of benefits to individuals and communities as it empowers people to have more say over their daily lives. However, in the context of wider integration, civic participation also provides valuable opportunities for meeting and engaging with people from different backgrounds, which in turn can help build trust and cohesion within communities. This link is well recognised by policy makers but is yet to be translated into action on the ground. The recent inquiry into local government by Sir Michael Lyons explicitly identified the connection between fuller participation rates and greater community cohesion in an area.[1] Similarly, the Commission on Integration and Cohesion calls for local areas to develop a "shared future",[2] and the report and the recent local government white paper both stress the need to have "safe" public spaces where issues of difference can be debate and explored.[3]

These goals can only be realised if individuals feel that their voices will be listened to and that they can shape debate. A shared future can only be achieved if all communities within an area are able to take part in the process by which that future is discussed and agreed. If you consistently exclude a group or groups from the processes by which society functions, then they are bound to have less positive opportunities and life experiences. Hence, active and inclusive participation, alongside equality of opportunity, is a prerequisite for overcoming difference and building tolerance.

Later in this chapter we spell out what this might mean in both formal and informal settings. Inclusive participation matters both in the formal decision-making processes and in the more informal social networks that in reality govern much of any individual or community's daily experiences. The fact remains, however, that in too many cases, cohesion is seen as an add-on issue and not related to mainstream activity such as community engagement and involvement. Government at all levels needs to make the connection and realise that you cannot build cohesion and integration without participation.

Making the connection

As mentioned above, several important policy documents over the past couple of years have emphasised the value of participation to both individuals and communities. Although most of the evidence to support these claims is anecdotal, there is a compelling and growing body of case studies that demonstrate how working together towards a shared goal contributes to building cohesive and mutually respectful communities. One such example, listed in the Commission on Integration and Cohesion's recent report, is the Walker area in Newcastle. Walker is a traditionally white, patriarchal, working-class area that since the decline of industry has suffered high levels of unemployment and poverty. As traditional communities have moved away from the area, new groups have arrived. This has led to tensions between long-term residents and newcomers, many of whom are of a different religious or ethnic background from the established population. However, this situation has been turned around through persistent attempts by local organisations and community activists to bring new and established groups together to tackle local problems. This has included the highly acclaimed "Images for Change" project, which gave residents disposable cameras to document aspects of their community they were particularly proud of or keen to change. The Commission on Integration and Cohesion concludes that these initiatives have contributed to "revitalise local residents' sense of community pride", encouraging them "to come together over shared principles and commonalities … welcome changes and work towards improving their local area".[4]

However, although the success of initiatives such as this is well recognised among policy makers, the link between participation and cohesion is not always made on the ground. Moreover, the UK has a long way to go before all groups in society feel able or willing to take active part in the civic or community life around them; levels of participation still differ widely between social groups.

Democratic legitimacy

A key touchstone in terms of how different groups participate is the inclusion of minority communities in elected or decision-making institutions. If we were to adopt the American revolutionary maxim of "no taxation without representation", many of our communities could rightly feel thoroughly disenfranchised. At the centre of our democracy, the House of Commons would need to have over 60 ethnic minority MPs rather than the current 15 to be truly reflective of Britain today. It is troubling that, in terms of minority representation, the House of Lords is currently more representative of Britain in the 21st century than the Commons.

This pattern of unequal participation is reflected at local level. Too many of our local authorities continue to reinforce the stereotype that they are "pale, male and stale". This is a challenge for our political parties. They need to look at their memberships, their activist bases and their procedures and ask themselves very hard questions about why they do not seem to be able to welcome ethnic minorities into their ranks and promote those that are there. They must also resist the temptation to ally themselves with one particular minority community in order to gain a local advantage – that is the tactic of those at the margins of the political debate and not worthy of any party that seeks to be in government at national, regional or local level.

However, in an age of increased devolution and localised decision making, it is important to look not just at elected bodies but also at those others that purport to be representative of an area and exercise power to divert resources and make decisions. Ethnic minorities are still grossly under-represented in a number of local institutions such as local strategic partnerships (LSPs), health boards, school governing bodies and cultural bodies.[5]

Social and civic inclusion

Outside the more transparent decision-making process of the country, we should not forget the immense influence that is wielded by informal networks and civic society. A key driver of the disparities that exist in this field is the pernicious intersection between race and poverty. The highest levels of participation can be found in the most prosperous areas, among the young and people with free time.[6] The lowest levels of participation are among the poorest in society, who are therefore deemed to be partly responsible for the disadvantages they suffer, as they cannot expect rights if they do not fulfil their responsibilities.

Research from the Commission for Racial Equality (CRE) shows just how profound an effect deprivation has on participation rates. For almost every type of civic participation, the top 10% most deprived areas in the country showed the lowest participation rates. The differences in participation rates were particularly stark for formal volunteering and neighbourhood activities. In addition, people living in the most deprived areas had less knowledge and enjoyment of civic participation activities than those living in less deprived areas. The barriers come from a lack of access and opportunities, driven by cultural, educational and physical barriers, such as the absence of community facilities and spaces for meeting. The link between deprivation and existing inequalities and lower participation rates makes exacerbated racial inequalities inevitable. When 70% of people from ethnic minority communities live in the 88 most deprived wards in England,[7] the current climate is effectively disenfranchising the majority of our ethnic minority communities.

Yet there is evidence that positive, inclusive participation can turn this situation around. An often cited success story is the Balsall Heath Forum in Birmingham. Like the Walker area in Newcastle, Balsall Heath tells a story of a traditional working-class area disrupted by the decline of industry and a fast-changing demography, which rediscovered its community spirit through bringing old and new residents together to shape the area in which they live. Primarily driven by grassroots activists and local faith organisations, Balsall Heath Forum has over a 25-year period transformed not only the look and feel of the area, but also the attitudes and behaviour of its residents. Ethnic and religious tensions have eased, house prices have gone up, the residents are proud of where they live; and over a third of the 12,000 population regularly take part in activities to improve their neighbourhoods.[8]

Choice and voice

Current political vogue dictates that service users require more choice and voice in how they access these services. Without wishing to get drawn into a semantic discussion over the differences between "choice" and "voice", it is important to be clear about the distinctions between them.

Voice should be about democratic legitimacy and formal involvement in decision making. Greater devolution should promote this and, provided it is founded on principles of inclusion and equality, more voice can be empowering. Indeed, the importance of an increased level of local engagement is one of the foundations of last year's local government white paper.[9] The government stresses the need to generate increased participation, all chiming with the desire for more voice in service delivery.

However, it is choice that is the policy of the moment: choice of the services we receive and the providers that deliver them. Yet choice can actually lessen participation and undermine moves towards greater equality. There is clear evidence that middle-class groups are better able to use choice schemes to their advantage,[10] and, as we have seen, deprivation and poor educational opportunities can dramatically reduce the likelihood of an individual participating in the society around them.

In this climate, both choice and voice are far more likely to be exercised by those who have the resources and predilection for wider community engagement. This means that the choice and voice agenda could further marginalise some communities. A recent research report published by the Joseph Rowntree Foundation explored participation and the "voice" of South Asian minorities in Bradford.[11] This work tried to explore why some voices were heard more easily than others and the effect of not hearing some of those voices. Among those who felt unable to have their voice heard feelings of powerlessness were significantly increased.

Hence, choice and voice policies need to be radically rethought if they are to avoid entrenching inequalities and actually lowering levels of participation from already excluded communities. There are many case studies of how giving traditionally excluded people a say in issues of importance to them can help overcome tensions within and between communities. One example is the Waltham Forest award-winning Defending Da Hood (DDH) project. DDH was set up to bring young people together to address issues relevant to them, with the aim to reduce gang-related crime and to improve the life chances of local youths.

The project, which consists of a number of initiatives, events and consultation activities targeted at young "hard to reach" people, has been praised for building trust between participants and creating better understanding and appreciation of young people and their needs in the local area.[12]

Clearly, having a say in how an area is run or a service is delivered can empower individuals and promote more cohesive communities; but the choice must be real, and sufficient advice, information and support must be available. Such measures as choice advisers, rigorous ethnic monitoring of decision-making processes, and specifically targeting excluded groups are essential if we are not to risk increasing the democratic deficit.

Discrimination and racism

In encouraging both formal and informal participation, ongoing inequalities and even outright discrimination and racial abuse are still significant barriers. As outlined above, many of the factors that provide the platform for meaningful participation in the governance and civic life of the country are still unevenly distributed between people.

For many ethnic minority communities, experiences of racism can be a significant barrier to civic participation. Forthcoming CRE research shows that overt racism and harassment is an expected part of the daily experience for many members of ethnic minority communities, and that they feel this to be the single most important factor restricting their full participation. Gypsy and Traveller communities, for example, consistently identify the extreme prejudice and persecutions which they face every day as the defining feature of their lives. For some religious communities, this has been exacerbated by the climate of fear around terrorism. Such entrenched racism excludes many people from participating in mainstream civic participation by eroding their confidence, reducing their morale and perpetuating their exclusion.

Yet in some communities this can be a motivating factor for greater involvement. A recent example of this has been the recent increase in the number of Muslim groups that have been engaging in public consultations and debates post the 7/7 bombings.

Conclusions

As we have seen, unequal levels of participation, both formal and informal, are a vicious cycle that leads to increased disempowerment and inequality. New moves to encourage wider engagement and participation may well only serve to exacerbate this situation unless the cycle is broken. It is clear that Britain's ethnic minority communities are under-represented in the corridors of power, be they national or local. They are also less likely to have their voices heard in influential social networks or the more subtle forums where power is exercised. Much of this is not through any desire to exclude or discriminate. It is the legacy of past wrongs and prejudices, which have left many of our ethnic minority communities without a platform to influence the society around them.

Correcting this requires huge political will and effort. Our parties must be more open and inclusive and seek to ensure that they are truly representative of the wider population. However, we must also ensure that our systems and decision-making processes are more open and inviting. Choice and voice must apply to everyone and not just to those who can manipulate the system to their advantage. Existing forms of participation do not promote equality and need changing, not simply devolving to an ever-more local level. Increased voice in how decisions are made, how money is spent and how services are run is vital to ensuring better decision making, wiser use of resources, more satisfactory services and the creation of a more equal Britain. As the examples listed above have shown, it is also a necessary step to creating more cohesive and mutually respectful communities. For this to happen, that voice needs to be inclusive and representative of the country as a whole. We cannot rely on existing power structures or the more informal channelling of influence to make the best decisions for multi-ethnic and multi-faith Britain. If we are to have a truly "participation nation", the whole nation must be able to take part and that means we need to change the way participation happens to make it more open, attractive and inclusive. This is not just vital for the sake of it. Achieving cohesion and integration depends on all communities being able to participate. Without that, we will not become more equal and we will reduce the number of opportunities for interaction and the inclination of citizens to participate in the wider community.

Notes

1   Lyons inquiry. 2007. *Lyons inquiry into local government: final report*. London: Stationery Office.

2   Commission on Integration and Cohesion. 2007. *Our shared future*. London: Department for Communities and Local Government (DCLG).

3   Ibid; and DCLG. 2007. *Strong and prosperous communities: the local government white paper*. London: DCLG.

4   Commission on Integration and Cohesion. 2007. *Our shared future*. London: DCLG; and Commission on Integration and Cohesion. 2007. *Integration and cohesion case studies*. London: DCLG.

5   See for example the Commission for Racial Equality's recent research on participation and local strategic partnerships: Black Training and Enterprise Group and Urban Forum. 2007. *Participation and local strategic partnerships*, London: CRE.

6 Ibid.

7 Social Exclusion Unit. 2004. *Taking stock and looking to the future: emerging findings*. London: Social Exclusion Unit.

8 http://www.balsallheathforum.org.uk. See also Blunkett, D. 2003. *Active citizens, strong communities – progressing civil renewal*. London: Home Office.

9 DCLG. 2007. *Strong and prosperous communities*.

10 Social Exclusion Unit. 2004.

11 Blakey, H., Pearce, J. and Chesters, G. 2006. *Minorities within minorities: beneath the surface of South Asian participation*. York: Joseph Rowntree Foundation.

12 http://www.nya.org.uk/Templates/internal.asp?NodeID=95393

Learning to participate: reflections on the work of innovative schools

By Valerie Hannon

How are the habits of participation in the public realm established? It is reasonable to assume that early experience of personal agency affects an individual's disposition to engage and contribute. Experience when young of influencing key aspects of one's own life and its social conditions may be an important predisposing factor. So too the arena of schooling ought to be one where we pay special attention to the scope for the fullest engagement and influence of young people themselves, both for its own sake and for its establishment of habits and expectations in adult life. Yet if learning is one of the most human, developmental and growthful things we do, how is it that the experience of schooling nevertheless remains alienating for a substantial proportion of the recipients of it? The solution has always been known by skilful and gifted educators to lie in engagement and ownership by learners. The problem has arisen in seeking to achieve this on a mass, compulsory, industrialised scale. And it has been further compounded by the intense pressures of globalisation, where the imperative to raise standards for economic survival has been experienced by both the educators and the learners as one of standardisation. Perhaps the problem lies in the very concept of compulsory education in itself. But the notion that deschooling might be the solution has not been seriously debated since the days of Ivan Illich,[1] albeit that organisations like the OECD, in its *Schooling for Tomorrow* project, developed a futures-scenario focused on deschooling as a clear possibility. [2]

In one sense, non-participation is easily quantifiable. "Unauthorised absence" – truancy – in 2006 stood at 55,000 young people missing lessons every day. Moreover it would appear to be rising not falling. The official figures for truancy rates have risen from 1.2% to 1.42% of the secondary school population between 2005 and 2006. In 2005-2006, 7% of pupils at secondary school were persistently absent from school during the academic year, missing 35% of their lessons, by either playing truant or because an absence had been approved beforehand.

This is has occurred during a tough official crack down on truancy, with fines up to £2,500 or three months in prison for parents who fail to improve the attendance of persistent truants in the course of 12 weeks.

In another sense, participation – or lack of it – is harder to calibrate. For many young people, physically turning up at school is by no means the same thing as being present. The percentage of students (without any special learning difficulties) who ended 11 years of compulsory schooling in 2006 with no qualifications to show for it was 2.7%. That is over 20,000 young people.

The percentage who achieved at a dismal level (fewer than five GCSEs at grades A–C) was 21.4%. It is safe to assume that these young people have not felt a powerful sense of ownership or engagement in the educational experience; perhaps not many of them would call it a "learning journey".

Even among those who do achieve, the most common adjective used by young people in relation to schooling is that it was "boring". Further evidence, if any were needed, that the schooling industry has a problem, lies in the rise of home education (within the law since the 1944 Act).

Estimates of the number taking this option for England and Wales range from 12,000 to 84,000, which would be about 1% of the school population. At the moment, however, there is wide agreement that this category is likely to continue to grow. The home education group Education Otherwise says hits on its website have quadrupled in the last year and the annual growth in home education could now be 20%.

However, rather than walking away from the education service, increasing numbers of users and educators are seeking to reinvent it. The main thrust of government policy has, naturally enough, focused on service improvement through the usual toolkit of increased accountability as well as investment, consumer choice and the levering up of professional standards. However, within the service, in schools up and down the country, people are turning to approaches that focus on student voice, co-creation and co-production in the learning business. The question is: are services merely to be "delivered" to a set of consumers, however well differentiated, or are they to be produced by the innovative participation of those who need and want them? The first step is to enable users' voices to be heard.

The government is not oblivious to the need. In 2003 the DfES publication *Building a culture of participation*[3] aimed to provide ideas and give guidance to a wide range of organisations, including schools, about how actively to involve young people within services and policy making. It focused on how to listen to children and young people so that their views would bring about change. Moreover, almost every major support agency in the education world now has some programme to assist schools to develop their processes to enable authentic student voice, through school councils, student governors, youth parliaments and so on.

An advanced example is to be found in the Weston Federation of Schools in North Somerset. This partnership has created a student parliament, with representation from each of the six school councils involved. The young people are able to inform and challenge the Federation's thinking – they attend Federation leadership and governors' meetings, undertake research, contribute to school self-evaluation strategy and practice, and contribute to staff training sessions. This type of engagement will enable young people to become confident leaders of learning.

Networks of schools are supporting each other in deepening these approaches.[4] And of course students themselves have taken a lead with the establishment of the English Secondary Students Association (ESSA), which promotes the benefits of young people becoming part of the decision-making process that affects their school lives. It provides individual students with support for voicing their views and opinions. Among other things, ESSA has produced the *Learner Voice Handbook*.[5] The first London Student Voice conference was held in June 2006. The event was put together by members of London's Student Voice steering group and was attended by students and teachers from 56 London schools. Further events are now being planned.

Innovative practitioners in the learning sector want to go beyond existing models of "consultation" toward deeper engagement. In a wide range of projects the Innovation Unit is supporting practitioners to develop "next practice" in this field through a set of reflective field trials.[6] In one project, the local authorities of Bolton and Bedfordshire, widely recognised as developing children and young people's voice in various parts of their respective councils, are working together to take this work much further. They are supporting student action teams to work with adults to co-construct strategic leadership roles in the deployment and delivery of personalised services for citizens.

The student action team model engages young people in real decision making and action, which takes them beyond the classroom to work on issues valued by students and the broader community, and which are linked to other mandated curriculum and community goals. The field trial will empower children, young people and adults to work collaboratively to solve problems, make decisions and plan for their collective futures. It will also seek to challenge not only what is within the traditional "school" setting with a drive towards personalisation, but also what the wider council services, under Children's Services with its Every Child Matters agenda, are doing to ensure the personalisation of the whole system.

A similar process is under way in Hartlepool. Leadership in such deprived areas is always tough so engaging genuine local leadership and empowering it is a further challenge. Local issues in North Hartlepool are being tackled by traditional methods but improvements have reached a plateau and need new approaches. The North Hartlepool Extended Services Partnership (NHESP) is developing a network of community leaders – adults and young people – who will be empowered to lead the development of extended service provision.

This work will explore a new form of governance through a "brokerage board", comprising community partners, the local authority, a local voluntary project centre, the Children's Fund, and representation from seven local primary schools and one comprehensive secondary school.

The aim is to create a personalised, multi-agency and community-driven approach to meet the needs of learners of all ages, focusing on well-being and self-esteem. Key to this process is the intention to bring together people from different backgrounds with a wide range of skills and experience and with fresh perspectives to contribute. The Partnership hopes to provide a model of leadership that realises the potential of the area's social, material and intellectual capital.

Supported by the Innovation Unit and the National College for School Leadership, the Partnership has held a scoping event to allow a range of services, including schools, to describe their work, targets and priorities for the North Hartlepool area and to look for common ground. A community event attracted a very wide audience of professional, community and family representatives. There was widespread agreement that nothing like it had happened in Hartlepool before, still less in that locality, and enthusiasm to carry the ideas forward was enormous.

Innovations such as these represent attempts to push the boundaries of the ways in which user voice is not just heard, responsively or not, but empowered. Nevertheless the experience of leadership and governance is not one that everyone chooses, even under highly facilitative conditions. The challenge for *all* learners is how to be enabled to be co-producers of a learning journey that is engaging and relevant, as well as rigorous, appropriately challenging, and enabling. Here the innovators are moving beyond the efforts to personalise learning through improving choice. They are incorporating, as a matter of course, techniques such as assessment for learning, student researchers, "learning walks" and peer coaching. Through these methods, students *own* their learning objectives and progress in significant ways.

Crosshall Junior School in Cambridgeshire is seeking to find out how starting the project from the interests and concerns of the pupils will influence the style and content of the curriculum. Their project asks whether the depth of learning will increase when children engage in the planning process of their learning journey. Their Innovation Unit-supported field trial includes the full range of abilities within the whole of Year 5. The school will open on Saturdays to allow families, and fathers in particular, to support their children in using information and communication technology (ICT) and see what they are working on as part of the field trial. Resources will be prepared to support children in pursuing their own learning journeys and to extend their learning at home.

The project is characterised by pupils' genuine and active participation in decision making and learning co-design, and has a number of strands. It will start with a module from the humanities and enable pupils to be the leaders of their own learning via two methods. In one, pupils will have access to an overview or mindmap of the whole module to be covered, and be able to dip in where they choose. In another, pupils will start with an investigative question which could be context, challenge or "big picture"-based, co-constructing learning pathways with teacher facilitators who will play to their own particular strengths and skills.

Pupils will also participate in activities traditionally associated with teaching as they set their own targets, understand where they need to go next, and create resources through their interactions with other children. The project is marked, additionally, by a sense of moral participation, or selflessness, in pupils who recognise their own skills, and their responsibility to share and encourage those skills in others. The school's personalisation in practice aims to develop articulate and reflective learners to become active in their choice of resources, able to evaluate the choices they make, knowledgeable about their own skills and values, and more self-confident in expressing their needs to a Year 7 teacher.

Finally, the innovators and activists in this field find their efforts now being turbo-charged by the possibilities of the new technologies, and young people's familiarity with it, which usually far outstrips that of their teachers.

Wildern School in Southampton is encouraging students' participation in learning through the use of new technologies with which young people are familiar outside the school context. The school is using its virtual learning environment (VLE) to create its own secure version of YouTube, a large-scale, user-submitted online video/audio repository for education. A group of students has access to specialised training in story boarding and film-making techniques, plus digital cameras and microphones for filming, and i-macs for editing out of school hours. They are working together in small teams with two other untrained students, to create education resources in audio and video formats.

Students are actively creating and rating learning resources. Student panels in each year group are responsible for quality assuring the outputs, reviewing and rating the videos submitted by that year group before they are uploaded on to the site. Participation in this kind of approvals process enables students to experience assessment for learning, provides them with access to the school curriculum, and improves their critical thinking skills and teamwork. They are asked to engage in peer assessment via ratings and monthly awards for best of category, and there is an Oscar-style ceremony with prizes for the best films. In a newly opened community cinema on the school site the films voted best in their category are shown to the community before the start of the main feature film. Currently, the project involves Wildern and its eight feeder primary schools. Within two years it could also include the 35 schools for which Wildern provides the VLE.

How far can these moves be taken? The answer to this may lie in the degree to which the untapped potential of families is realised. That engagement in their children's learning journey should decline to the point of extinction after primary school is clearly a massive waste. Maybe the shape of things to come can be discerned as is so often the case at the edges – in the experience of the excluded.

The Bridge Academy is a pupil referral unit in Fulham, London. In an IU-supported field trial, which has been running since autumn 2006, staff are seeking to change the nature of the way its students participate in learning. The Bridge Academy Online is the school's locus for innovation, and involves redesigning workforce roles, the curriculum and organisation of the school. It has drawn inspiration from Stephen Heppel's work and website Notschool.net.[7] The Bridge will set up a differentiated core offer to enable it to provide for students outside the confines of the school building and school day. This offer ranges from a five GCSE diet to a highly individualised offer, which includes (accredited) work and tailored courses. In phase 1 of the project, the Academy is providing 16 of the Year 9 students with an ICT equipment package, online activities and support for themselves and their families. By changing the timetable so students work from home for a day a week, it allows time for students to undertake these activities, and for teachers to personalise their learning.

Where home-based kit has been provided, and one day working from home is being trialled, families have created a learning space in the house that was not there before, where technology and social learning is working together. The "kit" gives the school a hotline into living rooms, inviting parents and siblings into learning, while visits to students' homes to install the equipment have given staff added insight into their students' lives and interests. Those involved in the trial expect to see the role of teachers and mentors change radically as they become experts at creating digital assets that underpin learning and guide families towards educational achievement. A launch event achieved 90% attendance for Year 9 students, compared with very low attendance figures at a recent parents' evening for Years 8 and 10. Phase 2 of the project will involve all 175 students at The Bridge Academy.

The examples described above model emergent forms of participation and engagement in school-based learning which have transformational potential.

On a continuum they include the development of opportunities for young people:
—   to be leaders of learning
—   to exercise authentic influence in social organisations, and beyond schools across communities and localities
—   perhaps most significantly, to engage in the construction and design of their own personal learning experience.

Of course they raise some important unresolved issues which, though not new, need to be reframed and debated. For example, in our knowledge society, how do we get the balance right between the role of the state in setting frameworks, such as a national curriculum, and growing user co-creation?

The case studies of the innovators described above are not isolated examples, but are embedded in growing communities of practice. Nor should they be viewed as parallel to, or distinct from, the drive to raise standards. On the contrary, these approaches are increasingly being seen as holding the key to overcoming the current plateau in standards which has been reached through focusing on the supply side – teacher skills – and insufficiently on the demand side. They excite teachers, learners and their families alike. Like all innovations, they will probably pass from being regarded by some audiences first with ridicule, then with violent opposition – and, finally, as self-evidently sensible. Alongside these practical developments, however, we need to be prepared to address once more some fundamental issues of a more theoretical nature about the roles of the state, the users and the professions in education. It is an overdue debate.

Acknowledgements

Thanks to the schools and local authorities mentioned in this chapter who generously took time to describe their work; and to members of the Innovation Unit for their comments and contributions, particularly Grace Comely, Kirsten Hill, Denis Mongon and David Jackson.

Notes

1. Illich, I. 1971. *Deschooling society*. New York: Harper & Row.
2. National College for School Leadership (NCSL), Demos, Department for Education and Skills (DfES) and OECD. *Schooling for tomorrow: OECD Scenarios*. London: NCSL.
3. Kirby, P., Lanyon, C., Cronin, K. and Sinclair, R. 2003. *Building a culture of participation: involving children and young people in policy, service planning, delivery and evaluation*. DfES and National Children's Bureau.
4. See for example http://www.leadingintolearning.org.uk/pupilvoiceactivities.htm for the Blackburn and Darwin networked learning community schools' work on this.

5. ESSA and Futurelab. 2006. http://www.futurelab.org.uk

6. See http://www.innovation.unit.co.uk for information on the Innovation Unit; and Hannon, V. 2007. *Next practice in education: a disciplined approach to innovation*. Innovation Unit.

7. See http://www.notschool.net

Creating a climate for participation; global warming, the public and the search for elusive solutions

By Tony Juniper

It was not so long ago that a run of the mill article about climate change left the reader wondering whether or not to even worry about it. Couched in "ifs", "buts" and "maybes", non-specialist writers in particular treated the question of human-induced global warming as a finely poised debate. Although the science has for a long time told a different story, many media outlets have perpetuated unwarranted doubt about the urgent need for action.

Rapidly rising concentrations of greenhouse gases in the Earth's atmosphere have already caused average temperatures to rise, in turn leading to climate changes that are causing a wide range of profound environmental, social and economic impacts. The issue is not now about whether we are changing the climate, the crucial question is at what point will catastrophic climate changes be unleashed, leading to severe ecological change, humanitarian crisis and sharply escalating financial costs.

The answer to that appears to be "very soon indeed". Based on the latest modelling of climatic responses to the build up of greenhouse gases, it is now widely believed that the total warming caused by human activity should to be kept below a maximum of two degrees centigrade global average increase compared with pre-industrial average temperatures. If the world continues to emit greenhouse gases at the present rate, then the build up of carbon dioxide and other warming agents will reach a level that has an estimated 50% chance of taking us above two degrees within the next decade or so.

A ten-year window to stand an even chance of breaching the critical temperature threshold is not a comfortable position to be in. It is, however, the best guess we can make of where we have reached, and of where we are going. It might be even worse than this, or it might be better. It is about risk, and the higher the concentrations go, the more risky will be our climatic future.

Above two degrees, economic damages are expected to be severe, for example because of the effects of storms and floods. The melting of the Greenland ice cap becomes more likely and is expected to happen much faster above two degrees of warming. This on its own would add seven metres to global sea levels, spelling disaster for many of the world's largest cities, including New York, London and Shanghai, and leading to the loss of some of the world's most productive farmlands. Humanitarian impacts will most likely escalate as well, for example as a result of the impacts of drought on already marginal subsistence farming. More and more species will face extinction as average temperatures creep inexorably upwards.

Perhaps worse than this is the high risk of a series of positive feedbacks being triggered. For example the melting of the Arctic ice is already leading to more of the sun's energy to be absorbed by the now exposed dark surfaces of sea and tundra, whereas before some 90% of solar energy was reflected back into space by the vast expanses of pure white. The more it melts, the warmer it gets.

There is also the real prospect of large scale forest dieback, leading to the release of vast quantities of carbon dioxide into the atmosphere, thereby adding to the elevated levels of this gas already caused by the combustion of fossil fuels. Climate models show a considerable risk of changed rainfall patterns transforming the dense rainforests of the Amazon basin to savannah and even grasslands. The melting of permafrost is already leading to the release of carbon dioxide and methane (a far more potent greenhouse gas) and this is expected to be a major new source of global warming gases as more and more of the tundra turns from solid icy lands to spongy moist bogs.

Some of this prognosis used to sound like science fiction. It is now the scientific mainstream. Getting anything done about it is, however, very challenging. Certainly one aspect of what is needed in order to galvanise action is broader and more intense public participation. The first step in making that happen is to ensure that people are given the correct information and a fair assessment of what the latest science says.

Even now, even when the consensus in the specialist scientific community could almost not be stronger, minority voices are still printed and broadcast as though there is still a raging debate as to the reality of human-induced global warming. Even when the challenge is accepted, some seek to mislead the public as to the nature of scale of action that is necessary.

Considering the grave dangers now faced by life on Earth, and the impact continuing confusion creates on the political process, some editors and commissioners of programmes and articles need to wake up to what they are doing. So do the advertising firms who craft the misleading green propaganda that keeps big polluters in lucrative business. Certainly there is a vital need to maintain an open public debate on the science, and more importantly what to do about it, but pretending there is still serious doubt as to the basic scientific facts is clearly now an unwarranted and irresponsible distraction. So is the promotion of false solutions, such as "low emissions" vehicles that are actually nothing of the sort.
One survey of more than 900 peer-reviewed scientific papers concerned with climate change found that none disagreed with the basic science. By contrast the media has until recently (and in some cases still does) treated the science as an

open debate. The media's notion of "balance", when it comes to science, is often not appropriate. And yet the basic facts are still challenged, often by people with few relevant specialist technical qualifications.

The confusion that has (deliberately or not) been generated about the scale of threat and the solutions to it is a real barrier to the effective public participation that is now vital in avoiding the worst effects of human-induced climate change. That participation must now be quickly moved into a public debate about what to do, not continually to debate whether or not there is even a problem.

So what will make the breakthrough from denial and confusion to engagement and substantive action? A major part of the solution is for there to be effective public participation. This can only be nurtured on the basis of clear and consistent information, however.

Many of the voices creating confusion and delaying action have vested interests to protect. Car, oil and coal companies have for example been among those funding campaigns to caution against early action. Some of them, having now been forced into accepting that there is a problem, are now engaged in various forms of "greenwash" (a term used by campaigners to describe undeserved, misleading or false green claims). Others have political views that see environmental protection as harmful to human development and object in principle to pollution control and other actions.

These sources of confusion and denial have already caused serious delay in bringing forward action and continue to stymie effective participation. I speak at many public meetings and my experiences at these gatherings confirm that there is a continuing and consistent level of debilitating confusion. Sometimes the confusion feeds a willingness for denial that is borne out of fear of what effective action would entail, for example less flying and other changes to consumerist lifestyles. Far easier to deny the problem than to change one's holiday plans, it seems.

But what steps can lead to a more informed public discussion about the basic science? Government has a role, for example in setting out clearer standards for green claims made by advertisers. Editors have a role, too, not least in taking urgent stock of their commissioning decisions and to look closely at what the science actually says. If, for example, there really was a conspiracy by the scientific community to mislead us all into wrongly believing that greenhouse gas emissions are linked to global warming, then of course that should be exposed. It should, however, be exposed on the basis of evidence, not simply opinion or a wish to deny what for some is an inconvenient truth. Confusing and damaging claims like this continue to be repeated, with not a shred of evidence to support them. How many editors of television channels and newspapers would seek out other scientifically unjustified opinions that might harm people?

If the subject were the effects of tobacco smoking or unprotected sex with strangers, a quite different set of norms would apply. Denying that smoking causes cancer or that AIDS can be transmitted through casual intimacy would be ruled out of order. There would be moral outrage. Placing millions of people at risk of food and water shortages, disease and the loss of their homes is by contrast regarded as part of a legitimate debate. The sooner this phase of the climate change debate ends, the more quickly we can ensure effective participation.

It seems that we would not normally expect the public to understand the arguments of other highly technical "debates" and to then make up their own minds about how to respond. In the case of tobacco very clear warning labels were placed on packs, while most forms of tobacco promotion has effectively been outlawed. In the case of AIDS, there were many official campaigns warning of the dangers of having unprotected sex, with advice about the need to use condoms. The confusion that has been deliberately generated in part explains why there are not yet warning labels on energy wasting cars like Range Rovers or advice warning of the consequences of flying. This is what we need, however.

We are moving toward the point that such actions might happen, but far too slowly. There is only now the narrowest window of opportunity and we need to make the most of it. This will require a much more frank interaction with the public by political and business leaders than has hitherto been the case. It will require that clear choices are set out and that the public is engaged in making those choices. This will not necessarily make for comfortable politics or marketing, but it is what our political and commercial leaders now need to do. In addition to clearer, more accurate and consistent information, we will need legal frameworks to make it clear what choices exist.

The latest science demands that countries like the UK achieve cuts in carbon dioxide emissions of at least 80% by 2050 (compared with 1990 emissions levels). This huge cut is feasible, but it will most likely not be achieved through the accumulation of many individual and voluntary actions. Recent history shows us some of the reasons why this is the case.

Since 1997 the UK has had an official target to cut carbon dioxide emissions by 20% by 2010 (compared with a 1990 baseline). This was a good target, but it won't be met. Indeed, in recent years, and following some initial success in cutting emissions, pollution levels have once again started to creep up. People are using more energy in the home, and more of that is produced from relatively more polluting coal compared with cleaner gas; we have more vehicles on the road and many of these are unnecessarily polluting. Not included in the estimates of overall carbon emissions are international shipping and aviation, but if they were included, progress toward meeting our target would be even worse.

The failure to meet even the relatively modest near-term targets is in part linked to how action in each sector is individually controversial and is not linked to the overall picture. Road fuel duties, air fuel taxes, curtailing road building, reducing food miles, energy efficiency standards for houses, phasing out energy-wasting products (patio heaters for example), changing the minimum fuel efficiency standards for vehicle engines, implementing large-scale renewable energy schemes (wind power in particular) and international treaties setting out which countries should do what by when have all been blocked, not only in part through the expression of doubts as to whether we even have a problem, but because each is unpopular and difficult and therefore something else should be done.

Anti-wind campaigners demand more energy efficiency, companies defend old inefficient technologies so as to protect profits and jobs, product standards are resisted because of the impact on choice, road charging is seen to be a limitation on freedom, aviation fuel taxes are resisted because they are claimed to be regressive, and so on and so forth. The result of all this is rising emissions, and not the dramatic cuts that are urgently demanded by the latest science. So how under these circumstances can more effective participation be secured? One important step is through the creation of a more effective framework.

Friends of the Earth has made the case for a legal duty on government to deliver annual cuts in emissions commensurate with the latest science. This would not end the controversy, but it would create the conditions under which more effective public participation could take place. If, for example, there is a major public and business rejection of demand management for the aviation sector, then the question would be automatically posed as to what other areas should instead deliver cuts. If we are to increase aircraft trips, then who else will ensure that we reduce by the necessary amount? Should it be the coal burning power stations, the manufacturers of products that waste power on "stand by", or car manufacturers, or should we build many more wind turbines? In other words the choices would become clearer and public participation would be all the more effective.

This won't happen if left to some form of "free market of ideas". The conditions for effective public involvement needs to be deliberately created by elected governments with the backing and cooperation of companies. At the time of writing the bill that could deliver an official requirement for emissions reductions is being debated by parliament. It could, if made tough enough, lead to a transformation in the public debate on climate change and how best to deal with it.

Public participation leading to widespread ownership of the solutions to climate change is an essential component of how we will move (or not) toward low carbon societies. That participation cannot be taken for granted, however, or left to poorly resourced environmental groups to muster. It needs to be deliberately nurtured by a wide range of actors, including socially responsible media editors, forward looking government and environmentally minded businesses. To give effect to public views there must be clear legal frameworks that in turn reflect the urgency of the climate change challenge and ensure that sufficient action is taken in time.

Participation and legitimacy: the case for good deliberation

By Viki Cooke

Opinion Leader has over a decade's experience in citizen engagement, developing new techniques that involve information, deliberation and discussion. Since organising Britain's first ever citizens' jury in 1994, we've run hundreds of deliberative exercises ranging from small-scale qualitative projects such as citizens' juries and collaborative workshops, through to large-scale projects involving over 1,000 participants and a mixture of qualitative and quantitative "deliberative polling" techniques. Deliberative events offer a way for people to engage in serious and detailed debates about technical and complex issues of policy, often with others who are very different from themselves. This discussion draws on our experiences over the years to offer some key principles that we've developed to make sure that participatory decisions are understood to be legitimate – both for those involved in making them, and for those who are affected by them.

The specific format of our deliberative events has varied enormously – depending on the scale, the topic, the location and indeed the budget. But underpinning all of them has been a concern to develop processes of public participation which guarantee, as far as possible, that the widest possible range of voices are given the chance to speak, are genuinely listened to, and are taken into account in the process of deliberation. While I do believe that public deliberation should become a commonplace of our political landscape, the methodologies discussed here are by no means supposed to be a cure-all form of participation and no one would argue that they should be applied in all cases. That said, I believe that the processes and principles that we have developed over the years speak to a more general set of principles that should be applied to the broad toolkit of participatory methods.

Policy decisions that involve public participation stand a better chance of being acceptable to those most affected by them, and of working in practice. When public participation is carried out well, the outcomes are understood to be legitimate by everyone involved precisely because as many points of view as possible were listened to and taken into account. However, even in a world of widespread consultation and public involvement, not everybody will be involved in every decision. The challenge, then, is to make sure that the processes that we have developed to ensure legitimacy "in the room" are also recognised as due process by everyone who might be affected by the outcomes of that deliberation.

The appetite for participation: opportunities and challenges

From when our bins should be emptied, to how we should reform our pensions system, political decisions are increasingly seen as more legitimate if the process has involved participation in one form or another. Despite clear evidence that people (and particularly young people) are turned off by Westminster-style politics, the British public shows great willingness to engage with, and participate in, political issues from the local and very local to the national and global. Opinion Leader's survey of non-voters at the last general election showed that when offered a list of issues (such as tax, the economy, the environment), and asked which "really mattered" to them, 94% chose three or more issues. Furthermore, 71% of non voters said they were likely to get involved in a process where they decided how and where local money is spent.[1]

The move "from deference to reference", and the increased demand for participation that has accompanied it, is to be welcomed.[2] These changes promise huge prizes in terms of the vibrancy, dynamism and responsiveness of Britain's public realm. They also offer opportunities for citizens to become engaged as never before: taking ownership and responsibility for their politics; developing a clearer understanding of the trade offs; and producing a deeper appreciation of, and respect for, the views of other citizens. But the legitimacy that has seeped away from our parliament in recent years isn't necessarily being recouped through the ad-hoc mechanisms of participation that dominate at the moment.

The problem is that, although the demand for participation has grown, the ways that we participate haven't really changed that much. Campaigns such as the recent e-petition against road pricing can create an appearance of fervent "public opinion" that elected officials are loath to ignore. However, public acceptance of (and obedience to) political decisions rests, in part, on the notion that multiple points of view were given equal consideration and that a decision doesn't simply represent the whim of the majority or of the powerful.[3] In political science speak, it's not just about the transparent aggregation of preferences, it's also about whose preferences they are, how they are formed, and what influenced their formation.[4] While MPs and councillors have never been perfectly inclusive in their deliberations, the (sometimes arcane and anachronistic) rules and procedures that characterise debate in parliament are often there to ensure that a government cannot take decisions without answering the concerns and issues that have been raised by the representatives of different constituencies and interests. A shift towards greater participation without careful consideration of who gets heard and how they are listened to could short-circuit that discursive element – leading to greater exclusion and marginalisation beneath a veneer of greater popular participation and stakeholder engagement.

The problem of leaving decisions to "those who show up"

From low cost activities such as signing petitions or mailing postcards, through responding to consultations or filling in questionnaires, right up to spending large amounts of time and/or money lobbying, running for office, or staging protests, many forms of participation involve some element of self-selection and not everyone gets to participate equally.

On the face of it, this doesn't appear to be a problem – those who care most about something will be those who put most effort into participating, and those who care least will choose to abide by their decisions. But academics have long recognised that participation doesn't work that way. Certain participants tend to have more say than others about "what needs to change";[5] smaller, well-focused groups tend to do better than larger popular groups;[6] producers tend to do better than consumers;[7] strength of feeling doesn't always translate into effective action;[8] participation can often be labyrinthine and institutionally complex; decision takers are often better at listening to some kinds of people than others; and issues are often framed in ways that exclude some concerns from the conversation completely.[9] In a situation where some people are more able to participate (and do so more effectively) than others, those who are excluded could well feel that decisions are imposed on them in an arbitrary manner and without any concern for their ideas and viewpoints.

For those who are seen as stakeholders, or who have the resources to get themselves heard, a participatory decision feels more legitimate simply because their views were taken into account (even if the decision doesn't go their way). But, without careful thought about how we encourage participation in the future, there is a danger that we could end up with what Yvette Cooper MP has described as a "conservative communitarianism" where local policy is decided by those who turn up, shout loudest and have most time and money to dedicate to their cause.[10] For those who didn't know how to get involved, weren't approached by the decision takers, didn't have the skills to link up with others who had the same views as them, or who didn't even feel that there *was* anyone who shared their opinion, the fact that other, better mobilised, voices were heard – that "participation happened" – may not be enough to make a decision that affects their lives seem legitimate.[11]

Legitimacy "in the room" – representation and inclusion

It is only if participation is truly representative, its outcomes a product of a genuinely inclusive debate, that it stands any chance of achieving a broader legitimacy. Regardless of whether they agree with the outcomes, participants should feel that the discussion took place on common ground where their views were respected, given adequate consideration and properly understood by other participants.[12] Opinion

Leader has developed a number of practical steps aimed at ensuring participants experience deliberation in this way. Broadly speaking, they can be divided into two areas: a concern for representativeness and a concern for inclusiveness.

Representativeness

A central purpose of deliberative processes is to avoid the ghettos of like-minded people that might characterise less structured forms of participation.[13] Diversity of viewpoints strengthens deliberation and deepens the inclusive nature of the process – the more opinions that are voiced and listened to, the more legitimate the outcomes of good deliberation. For these reasons exactly who participates is a central concern when running a deliberative exercise.

Although the most obvious way of avoiding dominance by vested interests of all kinds is through a simple random sample from the community in question, a number of problems arise, which demand a more nuanced approach, which combats self-selection and shows a concern for equal voice.

Combating self-selection

Because participation is not compulsory, self-selection can undermine a simple random sample, as those with most time (or who are able to take time off work) or who have the biggest axes to grind, will be more likely to show up.[14] In bringing together deliberative events, we have employed a number of techniques to overcome the effects of self-selection including using a stratified sample procedure, randomly selecting from within the pool of people who agree to be potential participants; broadening the self-selected pool by offering cash incentives to participants; and being as helpful as possible about issues such as travel, childcare and the timing of the event, in order to minimise the barriers to potential participants.

A concern for equal voice

An important aspect of the deliberative process involves people's exposure to the ideas and experiences of those who they might not normally come into contact with. It's important, therefore, to think about what it is that we want represented. Simply creating a microcosm of the "outside world" in the deliberative event is likely to replicate all of the social or cultural structures that define the contours of an issue when it is thought about in a non-deliberative setting. In some situations, a concern for equal representation may demand that some voices are over represented numerically in order to compensate for their historical lack of voice within a particular debate.

Inclusiveness

Although having a sensitive and thoughtful approach to representation is a good start, getting the right people in the room is only the beginning. The core claim made by champions of deliberative forms of participation is that it is the actual activity of deliberation which makes the outcomes legitimate.[15] Whether it's described as the movement from "me" to "we", the establishment of a common ground, or simply as the impact of "seeing one another" for the first time, good deliberation goes beyond an aggregation of opinions towards forging new preferences in the light of fair and mutual understanding.[16]

Fostering an atmosphere conducive to good deliberation demands careful thought and planning. Over the years, Opinion Leader has developed a wide ranging toolkit of techniques, which can be built into the organisation of an event, or drawn on ad hoc by facilitators. These processes seek to ensure that enough information is available to allow participants to engage in debate on broadly equal terms, and to develop an atmosphere in which the contributions of all participants are equally valued, listened to and understood.

Get everyone up to speed

All participants are given information to help them form their views. The aim is to provide a baseline of knowledge, possessed by everyone in the room, which includes the key issues that are informing the current debate. This could be done by giving a simple account of the facts around an issue, or it could involve the presentation of arguments from a range of perspectives. The information is carefully tested on members of the public before the event, and small-group facilitators aim to ensure that everyone in their group is up to speed.

Have clear aims and objectives

Clarity about what each stage of a deliberative event is supposed to accomplish, and about how the deliberative exercise will affect outcomes, is important in order to frame the debate in the room. A clear account of the questions that need to be answered – so participants understand what the deliberation is for – is essential for maintaining focus. The task-oriented approach is often accentuated by getting groups to report back after each short debate, developing a list of practical suggestions on which the whole room can later vote.

Provide neutral, skilled, facilitation

Securing fair and inclusive deliberation depends, most of all, on well-trained, sensitive and focused facilitators. The role is not a manipulative one – participants don't necessarily possess the skills of analysis, prioritisation and decision making necessary to think about complex public policy issues. Furthermore the deliberative setting is one that demands a degree of sensitivity and openness from participants, which may go beyond the way they act in everyday conversations.

Alongside recording the deliberation, the facilitator has a major role to play in establishing a common ground dynamic among participants, and in moving the group towards their objectives. Facilitators have to be very attuned to the "feel" of the group – addressing any inequalities that arise, teasing out different opinions, and ensuring that everyone in the group genuinely understands what the others are saying.

Towards a broader public acceptance

Taken together, the processes outlined above can go a long way towards making deliberative methods of taking decisions, ranking priorities, and changing policy legitimate in the eyes of those who took part. However, developing a broader public acceptance of participation will also demand that these processes are understood to be fair, inclusive and representative by those who have not experienced them directly. Broader acceptance of deliberative forms of engagement may well flow from greater public familiarity with the techniques involved. If, as I believe it should, deliberation becomes a commonplace part of the policy process in Britain, then the very fact that it is happening more often could go some way to legitimising its outputs. However, such initiatives are easily undermined and, once lost, public trust is difficult to regain. There are a number of potential pitfalls; ways of avoiding them are discussed below.

Avoid debate for debate's sake

Across our deliberative events, we have sought to combat people's scepticism about the value of their participation by giving a clear account of what a particular instance of deliberative participation is for, how it will perform that function, and what the outcomes will be in terms of policy. The independent report *Your health your care, your say* noted that, in their assessments of the project, participants stressed the "commitment from all those involved in commissioning and running the initiative to taking the input of the public very seriously", and their sense that the project "seems very far from the 'tick box' mentality of many consultations".[17] Avoiding the accusation of taking a 'tick box approach' is a key element in widening the acceptability of these forms of participation. The danger is that these types of participation will be used to apply a participatory gloss to decisions that have already been taken, or to delay the taking of a decision at a difficult time in the political cycle.

Be clear about the process

Public confidence in the integrity and fairness of a participatory exercise will depend on the extent to which politicians and decision takers ensure that the engagement does "what it says on the tin". Wide publicity about engagement followed quickly by the announcement of a policy decision can (and does) create the sense that a consultative process was nothing more than window dressing. In contrast, processes that involve participation from the start, and maintain a clear account of how that participation has improved and changed policy making at each stage, stand a much better chance of being seen as a genuine and valuable part of the process.

The role of participation does not always have to be decisive – deliberation can be used to inform policy priorities, determine policy content, make tough trade offs between objectives, improve the methods of delivery, or simply to understand the way an issue is lived by those directly affected. What is important is that the reasons that the debate is being held are made very clear and the impacts it will have are explicit from the start. Alongside this, we have found that people take involvement most seriously when there is a clear link to decision makers and where the participative exercise actually involves those who will eventually be making policy.

Keep standards high

An expansion of participatory processes could also lead to a watered-down version of the practices and techniques outlined above. If the facilitation becomes less expert, the procedures more mechanistic, or the concern for inclusion less sensitive to issues of power asymmetry, then the possibility that deliberation can become understood as due process in some form or other will be undermined.

Clearly not all participation will work, and the impact on policy will vary greatly across sectors, departments and regions. In view of the need to maintain faith in the integrity of participatory exercises, an important aspect will be the role of evaluation and learning as a means to ensure that participation is well planned, well executed and its impact well understood.[18]

Conclusion

Representative and inclusive participation involving members of the public has much to offer as a way of improving policy making in Britain. Public participation of many different forms can result in better policy, whether that be a more acceptable account of the priorities, a clearer sense of which trade offs matter, or a more nuanced understanding of how an objective should be delivered on the ground. But participation and engagement also offer the possibility of rejuvenating the public's sense of trust in and ownership of the democratic institutions that affect their everyday lives.

Getting this sort of result, however, demands that the integrity of a participatory process is manifest, both to those who are participating, and for those who weren't involved in a particular decision. Although the methods outlined above are often specific to deliberative forms of engagement, the broader concerns – for representativeness, inclusion, clarity of process, and integrity of purpose – must be central considerations if participation in general is to become a legitimate and accepted part of our social and political life.

Notes

1. Opinion Leader Research conducted 1,025 interviews with people who were registered to vote but did not vote on 5 May 2005 (fieldwork date: 9–17 May). The research was conducted for the Power inquiry.
2. Watts, Kate. 2003. *The power of influence in the age of reference*. Admap, September.
3. Habermas, J. 1996. *Between facts and norms: contributions to a discourse theory of law and democracy* (translated by W. Rehg). Cambridge, Mass: MIT Press.
4. Sunstein, C. 1991. Preferences and politics. *Philosophy and Public Affairs* 20(1):20.
5. Richardson, J.J. and Jordan, A.G. 1979. *Governing under pressure: the policy process in a post-parliamentary democracy*. Oxford: Martin Robertson.
6. Grant, Wyn. 1989. *Government and industry*. Brookfield, VT: Gower Publishing.
7. Maloney, W. and Richardson, J. 1995. *Managing policy change in Britain: the politics of water*. Edinburgh: Edinburgh University Press.
8. Latham, E. 1952. *The group basis of politics*. Ithaca, NY: Cornell University Press.
9. Bachrach, P. and Baratz, M.S. 1962. Two faces of power. *American Political Science Review* 56(4):947–52. See also, Crenson, Matthew A. 1971. The un-politics of air pollution: a study of non-decisionmaking in the cities. Baltimore: John Hopkins.
10. Cooper, Y. 2004. The politics of localism. In Coles, J., Cooper, Y. and Raynsford, N. (eds) *Making sense of localism*. London: Smith Institute.
11. Carson, L. 2005. Avoiding ghettos of like-minded people: random selection and organizational collaboration. In Schuman, S. (ed.) *Creating a culture of collaboration*. Jossey Bass and Wiley.
12. Mansbridge, J., Hartz-Karp, J., Amengual, M. and Gastil, J. 2006. Norms of deliberation: an inductive study. *Journal of Public Deliberation* 2(1):1–47.
13. Sunstein, C. 2002. The law of group polarization. *Journal of Political Philosophy* June:175–95.
14. Carson, L. and Hart, P. 2006. What randomness and deliberation can do for community engagement. http://www.activedemocracy.net/articles/engag-comm.pdf
15. Cohen. 1996. Procedure and substance in deliberative democracy. In Benhabib, S. (ed.) *Democracy and difference*. Princeton, NL: Princeton University Press.
16. Ackerman, B. and Fishkin, J. 2004. *Deliberation day*. New Haven, Conn: Yale University Press.
17. Department of Health. 2006. *Evaluation of your health, your care, your say: an independent report commissioned by the Department of Health*. London: DoH, 78.
18. Warburton, D., Wilson, R. and Rainbow, E. 2007. *Making a difference: a guide to evaluating public participation in central government*. London: Involve.

Who benefits? The culture of public engagement

By Ben Page and Debbie Lee Chan

Over the last decade, consultants working on public engagement have never had it so good. There are now a veritable glut of agencies, consultants and experts that can be employed by public institutions to help them listen to and engage with their stakeholders on a range of service and policy issues.

Institutions themselves have been busy building up new structures to help them sustain engagement with stakeholders. Area forums, for example, are increasingly being introduced by local councils to bring people closer to public services operating in their neighbourhoods. In the health domain, provisions to engage with local people are being written into legislature in the form of Local Involvement Networks (LINks), which will replace the Patient and Public Involvement Forums (PPIFs) in 2008. Local police teams are running regular Safer Neighbourhood meetings at which the public set policing priorities. Even central government is at it, with the 10 Downing Street e-petitions website providing a state-sponsored mechanism through which large numbers of people can register their collective concerns about an issue at the touch of a button.

There is much to be positive about when we look back over the last ten years and see how much progress has been made in terms of the *way* public institutions engage with the public. For example, the trend for institutions to rely exclusively on postal citizens' panels as a major mechanism for engagement is dying out. In some cases, as much resource was spent on managing these panels as on actually listening to their membership. And the same is true of the PPIFs – with the new LINks there are moves to make patient involvement more mainstreamed and less confined to specific trusts or types of disease.

And let's not just focus on the change in tools and methods. The whole *culture* of engagement within many institutions has changed. More and more institutions are committed to engaging meaningfully with their stakeholders, not because they are obliged to by law or because this is what inspectors and auditors want, but because successful organisations do this. Camden Council is a glowing example of a local authority that has repeatedly stated this commitment and tried hard to deliver on it.

However, we also need to be honest about how much has been achieved. The maxim "Engage and they will come" doesn't always work. Despite huge efforts, the great British Public often refuse to show up to important consultation meetings, do not fill in surveys and fail to turn up to meet service providers when given the opportunity to do so. Officers often sit in empty community halls waiting for people to show up and tell them what they think, only to realise the public would rather watch the footie or *Big Brother*. It can be frustrating and time-wasting, and leads to disillusion.

To be more effective institutions need to be cannier in the way they engage with their stakeholders. This means looking at whether the processes and opportunities they are putting in place actually offer anything to the people they are meant to attract. It also means doing less but to a higher standard, and resisting the temptation to engage people over matters that simply aren't of any importance to anyone but the institutions themselves.

Lessons about improving public and stakeholder engagement
Here are some of the lessons we have learned over the years with regard to improving public and stakeholder engagement.

1. Most people want you to get on with routine business
We all have busy lives and we cannot expect people always to be involved with public services or to take an interest in every community issue going.

We've spoken to people about a variety of sectors, from health to policing and education, and almost uniformly find that they are more likely to want to know what's going on rather than always be actively engaged by service providers. This is not apathy: people simply want public services to get on with it. Of course there are exceptions – if people perceive something is going wrong they want to be able to tell you – but "if it's not broken, don't fix it" is by far the most common sentiment.

However, just because people don't want to be consulted *all* the time, it doesn't mean they think involvement mechanisms are a bad thing. Most want those opportunities to engage to exist even if they don't necessarily think they will use them. For many, these mechanisms play a reassurance role: they are nice to have, promising a way to change things and hold people accountable if required, but not something they expect to use regularly. This kind of attitude is typified by the survey results shown below, taken from a local residents' survey (Figure 1).

Of course even those who think they might be interested in getting involved are not necessarily going to find the time when it comes to it. In the above example just 2% of residents actually attended the forums once they were established. However, this is not necessarily a bad thing – it just means not everyone wants to be engaged all the time.

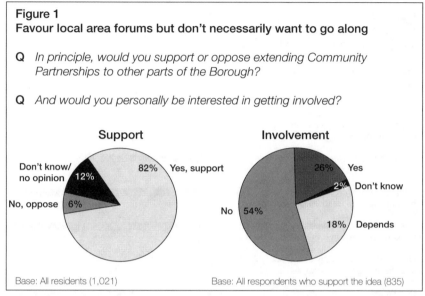

Figure 1
Favour local area forums but don't necessarily want to go along

Q   *In principle, would you support or oppose extending Community Partnerships to other parts of the Borough?*

Q   *And would you personally be interested in getting involved?*

Base: All residents (1,021)   Base: All respondents who support the idea (835)

2. Recognise that people should be allowed to get involved as and when they feel the need to be engaged

People like to get involved in a way that best suits them, at a time that suits them. It's a no-brainer. Which would you prefer to talk about – something that you frequently come into contact with, have a lot of experience of and can see ways to improve, or an issue you know nothing about, doesn't impact on you or your family and really is not that relevant to you?

In our Civic Pioneers research, councils that successfully engage residents feel strongly that it is important that mechanisms allow for people to engage on single issues – and suggest that although such issues can be used to draw people into engaging with them more generally, for most they are only ever going to want to engage in a piecemeal way. Similarly, the idea behind the new LINks in the health domain is that it operates like a loose network of interests and that different people will be active at any given time depending on their connection with the issue under consideration.

In some perverse way, it is sometimes not such a great sign that so many stakeholders want to engage with a particular institution all the time. This may be a sign that things are going wrong and they feel it is time to hold the institution to account. A good example of this point is taken from the London Borough of Hackney. As the council's performance improved, residents' desire to have more of a say declined (Figure 2).

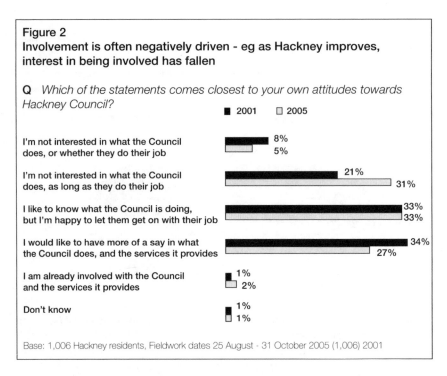

Figure 2
Involvement is often negatively driven - eg as Hackney improves,
interest in being involved has fallen

Q *Which of the statements comes closest to your own attitudes towards*
Hackney Council?

■ 2001   □ 2005

I'm not interested in what the Council
does, or whether they do their job
8%
5%

I'm not interested in what the Council
does, as long as they do their job
21%
31%

I like to know what the Council is doing,
but I'm happy to let them get on with their job
33%
33%

I would like to have more of a say in what
the Council does, and the services it provides
34%
27%

I am already involved with the Council
and the services it provides
1%
2%

Don't know
1%
1%

Base: 1,006 Hackney residents, Fieldwork dates 25 August - 31 October 2005 (1,006) 2001

We can tell from our extensive range of local authority survey data that lower satisfaction galvanises more people to want to make their voices heard. The chart in Figure 3 shows this inverse relationship between satisfaction and the desire to be involved.

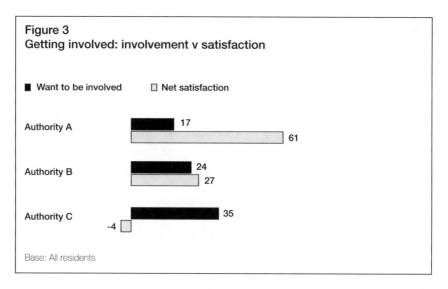

Figure 3
Getting involved: involvement v satisfaction

■ Want to be involved   ☐ Net satisfaction

Authority A   17 / 61

Authority B   24 / 27

Authority C   35 / -4

Base: All residents

Of course, we are not saying that you should provide a bad service just to increase public engagement, and we are not saying 5% response rates to surveys show you're doing a great job. However, we think it is important to recognise that lack of desire for engagement among the public or stakeholders is not always a bad thing.

3. Know what motivates people
We know not everyone wants to engage on every issue. But it is interesting to see, when they do engage, what motivated them to step forward. In our recent work on influence, one of the issues we explored was who gets involved in research and why. As can be seen in Figure 4, there's a difference between motivations of socio-political influencers (those who like to get involved and do so frequently) and for the general public as a whole. In particular, the top driver for socio-political influencers is the specific issue under debate – if it is important they will find the time, whereas for the public as a whole general curiosity about what the research is about is a key driver along with being asked to participate.

Figure 4
What motivated you to get involved in market or social research in the last two years?

	Socio-political influencer (base 171)* %	General public (base 1,666)* %
Felt that it was an important issue	67	34
The fact that someone asked me	59	49
Interested to see what I would be asked	57	52
Hoped that it would change something that directly affects me or my family	52	33
There was a financial incentive	41	39
Hoped that it would change something although it doesn't affect me directly	37	23
Caught me at a good time	30	24
Felt that it was my duty	27	15

* All respondents who have been involved

Source: Ipsos MORI

Of course, no single motivation is right or wrong. However, it is interesting that in a question where multiple responses were allowed, the socio-political influencers chose more reasons per person than the public as a whole. The influencers appear relatively active in their motives – it is all about impacting on important issues – whereas the general public appear more laid back about their reasons and are not as likely to be motivated by a need to change things.

The "sense of agency" issue is important. This is where officials and politicians can learn from the likes of Chris Martin or Bono, who can move millions of people to "Make Poverty History" by wearing a white wrist band. How does one make a community (even global) issue seem personal and motivate people to act? We think institutions will increasingly need to look to bring a sense of agency to the public that unites the spiritual and material sides of life – as E.M. Forster puts it, "only connect".

4. Understand that people want to get involved in different ways
What is key is that the latest wave of our audit of political engagement shows that political engagement has remained relatively stable since the first audit was carried out in late 2003. Although many people display an interest in local or national issues – while showing less enthusiasm for "politics" – far fewer are actually willing to become politically active.

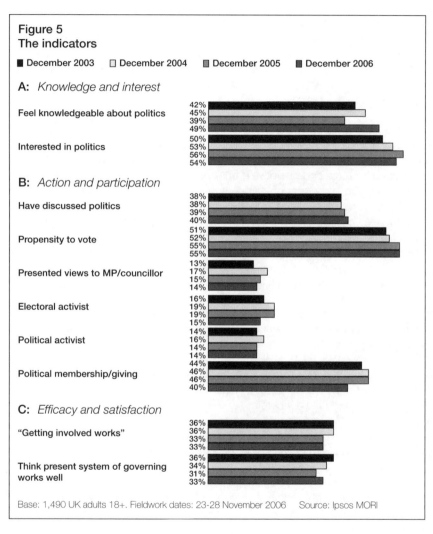

Figure 5
The indicators

■ December 2003 ☐ December 2004 ▨ December 2005 ■ December 2006

A: *Knowledge and interest*

Feel knowledgeable about politics
42%
45%
39%
49%

Interested in politics
50%
53%
56%
54%

B: *Action and participation*

Have discussed politics
38%
38%
39%
40%

Propensity to vote
51%
52%
55%
55%

Presented views to MP/councillor
13%
17%
15%
14%

Electoral activist
16%
19%
19%
15%

Political activist
14%
16%
14%
14%

Political membership/giving
44%
46%
46%
40%

C: *Efficacy and satisfaction*

"Getting involved works"
36%
36%
33%
33%

Think present system of governing works well
36%
34%
31%
33%

Base: 1,490 UK adults 18+. Fieldwork dates: 23-28 November 2006   Source: Ipsos MORI

The public do not just want to show their activism through formal mechanisms but through charity work, volunteering, joining groups of interest on the web, etc. People are involved in a wide number of community activities and simply don't want to express their concern for community issues through voting, formal meetings or formal decision-making processes – which can be very boring and potentially off-putting. In particular, people who have been to formal meetings often say they have been put off by the vociferous regulars who can dominate proceedings.

This means public services need to wise up to the fact that, like everything else in life, people want to have choice and flexibility in how they register their views on an issue and how they would like to contribute to their community. Public services will need to continue to highlight the numerous opportunities for people to have their say, particularly ones that are less formal and less likely to be perceived as party political.

5. Have a different conversation

This is one of our favourite phrases, because it encapsulates the growing trend for public services to have a genuine two-way dialogue with the public through participatory forums or deliberative events. At Ipsos MORI, we have seen a massive growth in the number of large and mid-sized events that bring the public and service providers together to have a creative and open dialogue. The success of these events also points to the fact that participants are very appreciative of the learning experience these events so often turn out to be. This learning is often a function of the information transfer that goes on during the events, to bring participants onto an equal footing with public service providers, and to help them deliberate on important decisions.

These quotes from participants illustrate that they feel they get a lot out of more engaging research events, and that they find it useful to have their views challenged:

> Very interesting … It made me think about issues that I hadn't
> really thought about before. And it was useful because I learned
> things I didn't know before.

> I found it intriguing and changed my own opinion on many
> occasions from hearing other people's views and the contrast of
> opinions from the group.

Also, if you play it right, engaging people effectively means they are more likely to be advocates of the research, and more likely to agree to participate again in the future:

> I found the workshop very interesting. Very much enjoyed being
> part of the discussion and would love to be present at another
> workshop in the future should the position arise.

However, to make these meaningful, participants need reassurance about what has changed as a result.

6. Communicate outcomes

Institutions need to demonstrate that they have *listened* to what people have told them and *considered* what they have heard. Public services are increasingly being obliged to do this, because this has been an area of weakness when it comes to public and stakeholder engagement. For example, things will change in the health sector soon as health bodies' duty to "involve and consult" will be extended to include the need for them to respond to local people, explaining what they have done as a result of what people have said throughout the year. Someone, somewhere, felt it was necessary to legislate for this.

Local government is a little ahead of the game in terms of informing people of the outcomes of consultation and engagement. Most local government websites list all past consultations and engagement exercises, and these lists sometimes but not always contain downloadable reports of results and outcomes. However, this is not always consistent across the board, and there is a whole world of communications beyond downloadable reports that should be used to let people know they have been listened to.

There is a myth that the public are some sort of angry mob who will rise up if crossed and therefore it might be better to not report when news is bad. The reality is, and we have seen this in deliberative events, that the public want to know what is going on and can cope with bad news. And to go back to our previous point, most of the time they simply want to be reassured that institutions have listened to their views and are now just getting on with business of taking them on board.

7. Be consistent

Finally, woe betide the organisation that attempts to remove engagement channels without careful planning and forethought. Public sector organisations across the country, from local councils to the Department of Health, have stories to tell about the upset that occurs if involvement mechanisms seen to be failing by government are shut down. To the minority who use them they are perceived to be a valuable way to have a voice, and even to those who don't use them, they serve as reassurance that, should they have a problem, there is somewhere to go.

In all this it is vital to consider what message *all* your actions are conveying, and if you do have a legacy mechanism that is not working as well as it could, it will require a high level of diplomacy to ensure a transition is smooth. Recently, our work with socio-political influencers has shown an overlap between those who get involved through traditional mechanisms and those who influence the attitudes and behaviours of their family and peers – suggesting that if you annoy the *usual suspects* it is likely that the negativity created will spread much further than you might originally expect. It is vital therefore to communicate positively why there is a need for change, and how people using the existing mechanisms will be able to keep making their valuable contributions.

So what does it all mean?

Ultimately, the moral is that the public don't see engagement as a good in itself. It's a means to an end – a way to change things for the better and hold organisations to account. If there's nothing wrong, it is not surprising that most people don't want to be involved.

Done well, harnessing the wisdom of users and their experiences always reaps dividends – but it is important to choose your battles. Think about the messages your organisation is sending out through its engagement mechanisms:

— Are you recognising the value of people's time (not necessarily financially, but at least by keeping things brief and targeted)?
— Are you using people's expertise (asking them about things they will be able to answer, enabling them to draw on relevant experience)?
— Are you giving people the chance to tell you what is important to them?
— Most importantly, are you committed to changing things as a result of your engagement with the public?

In summary, it's about quality not quantity; engaging people is important, but not if it's engagement for engagement's sake.

The timesqueeze generation: what the public are doing with their spare time

By Michelle Harrison and Michelle Singer

Introduction

"Time squeeze" was probably invented in the late 1980s. Originally associated with the Yuppy and fast-paced, affluent lifestyles, it quickly became a mainstream social trend. Because time squeeze has resulted from structural changes in British society, it is likely to stay around for the foreseeable future.[1] In 1997, 62% of people agreed that they "never have enough time to get things done"; in 2007, the number agreeing with this was 60%.[2] Over the last decade, the more affluent parts of British society have got used to spending money to save time, and have learned to value their time and energy more than their money.[3]

Insight into the lives and behaviours of the public is essential to the successful transformation of public services.[4] We need to understand more about how and why people are willing, or not willing, to engage. We need more knowledge on the potential opportunities to increase engagement and the barriers that need to be overcome, for different types of citizens and communities. In this chapter we draw on some recent work undertaken by the Institute for Insight in the Public Services (IIPS) on the British population and what we refer to as their "engagement profiles".[5] This has explored the role that time, energy and attitude all play in shaping peoples' engagement in the wider public realm: the types of household, community and public activities that they undertake in their every day lives and the views and aspirations that they have for participation in public life.

Time or energy: same difference?

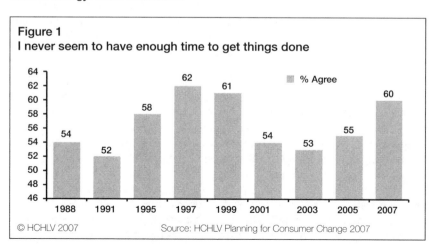

Figure 1
I never seem to have enough time to get things done

■ % Agree

Year	% Agree
1988	54
1991	52
1995	58
1997	62
1999	61
2001	54
2003	53
2005	55
2007	60

© HCHLV 2007   Source: HCHLV Planning for Consumer Change 2007

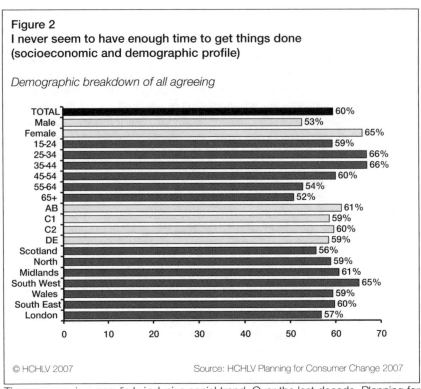

Figure 2
I never seem to have enough time to get things done
(socioeconomic and demographic profile)

Demographic breakdown of all agreeing

© HCHLV 2007   Source: HCHLV Planning for Consumer Change 2007

Time squeeze is a peculiarly inclusive social trend. Over the last decade, Planning for Consumer Change data shows that affluent people have felt a little more "time stretched" than less affluent people as a whole, but this is marginal. The business executive and the low income single parent juggling three jobs both feel under pressure.

There are consistent differences, however, between different groups within the population. Women feel much more pressured than men, while younger people, and particularly those of childbearing age, feel that they have less time available to them than older people. Parents feel more pressured than the childfree, and the most time pressured group in Britain are mothers who are in paid employment. None of this should be surprising but it is, as we explain later, important, for it influences the pattern of individual engagement in the public realm.

Over the last decade, "time squeeze" actually dipped for a number of years. Our qualitative research suggested that this was because people were getting better at coping with their changing social circumstances. Working mothers were finding it easier to get adequate childcare. Dads started doing housework. The number of domestic helpers, cleaners and gardeners grew exponentially, and the ready meal became a norm. At the Henley Centre we picked up on a cultural shift – instead of "stress envy", it became "cool to cope".

In parallel with this, we also noticed a new emphasis emerging from our qualitative research with the public. By the millennium, people were talking to us about how *tired* they felt. For some, it was a lack of energy, rather than a lack of time, that kept them glued to the sofa and the TV at night. A third of the population, apparently, were too tired to do anything else.

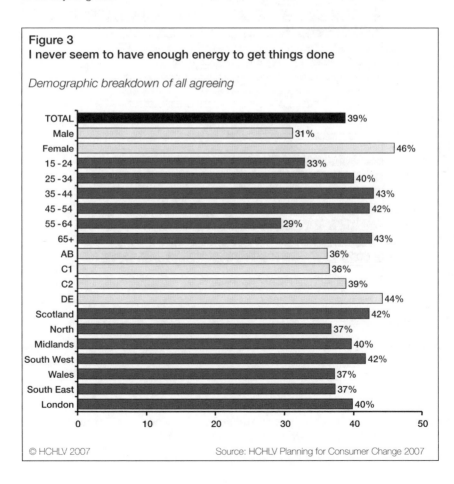

Figure 3
I never seem to have enough energy to get things done

Demographic breakdown of all agreeing

TOTAL	39%
Male	31%
Female	46%
15-24	33%
25-34	40%
35-44	43%
45-54	42%
55-64	29%
65+	43%
AB	36%
C1	36%
C2	39%
DE	44%
Scotland	42%
North	37%
Midlands	40%
South West	42%
Wales	37%
South East	37%
London	40%

© HCHLV 2007   Source: HCHLV Planning for Consumer Change 2007

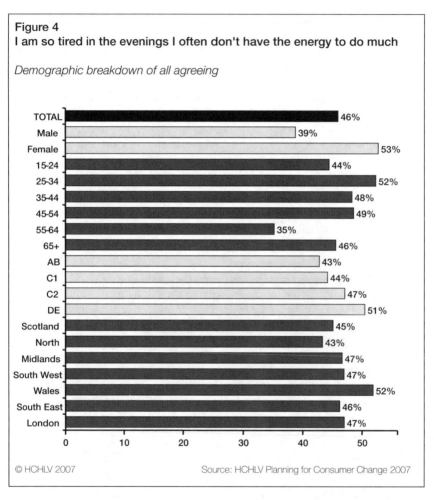

Figure 4
I am so tired in the evenings I often don't have the energy to do much

Demographic breakdown of all agreeing

TOTAL	46%
Male	39%
Female	53%
15-24	44%
25-34	52%
35-44	48%
45-54	49%
55-64	35%
65+	46%
AB	43%
C1	44%
C2	47%
DE	51%
Scotland	45%
North	43%
Midlands	47%
South West	47%
Wales	52%
South East	46%
London	47%

© HCHLV 2007   Source: HCHLV Planning for Consumer Change 2007

As with time pressure, this is more of a female trend. And, similarly again, those people in mid life (and more often those with children) feel it more. But there is also an important difference in profile between lack of energy and lack of time. Although time pressure is reasonably equitably distributed across the social classes, a *lack of energy* is disproportionately experienced by the poorest group in society. It is easy to dismiss this as a "soft" insight. But we believe this is a consequence of the vicious cycle of deprivation, as compared to the virtuous cycle of affluence (as we have written about in more detail elsewhere[6]). It also shapes the ability of people to engage.

Overall, one of the most important trends of the last decade for the 70% of society we can describe as "mass affluent" has been the decline in the importance of money. Peculiar as it may sound, when asked what resource they value most *in their everyday lives*, twice as many people will favour time over money; and a significantly higher number will favour energy over money. This is not the same for all social groups. Those of social group DE will, by virtue of necessity, value money more than their time and energy. Nearly half of those of social group AB, conversely, are willing to spend money to save time.

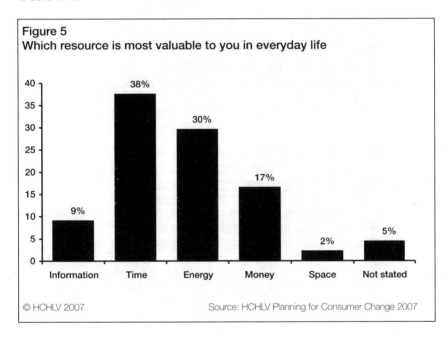

Figure 5
Which resource is most valuable to you in everyday life

© HCHLV 2007   Source: HCHLV Planning for Consumer Change 2007

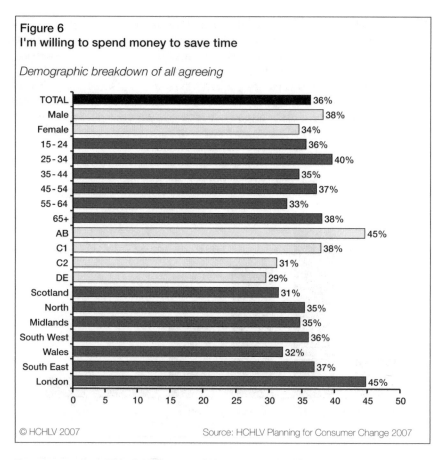

Figure 6
I'm willing to spend money to save time

Demographic breakdown of all agreeing

Demographic	%
TOTAL	36%
Male	38%
Female	34%
15-24	36%
25-34	40%
35-44	35%
45-54	37%
55-64	33%
65+	38%
AB	45%
C1	38%
C2	31%
DE	29%
Scotland	31%
North	35%
Midlands	35%
South West	36%
Wales	32%
South East	37%
London	45%

© HCHLV 2007   Source: HCHLV Planning for Consumer Change 2007

Engagement: profiling Britain

Against this background of understanding, we undertook more detailed research in the 2007 edition of *Planning for consumer change* to explore the extent to which time and energy were determining factors in the way in which people chose to participate in the public realm. This followed on from detailed work in 2006 on the future of citizenship, where we uncovered much public uncertainty around the concept and strong attitudinal barriers to engagement among lower income working people.[7] We were interested to understand more about the patterns that we had uncovered through our earlier qualitative research and, most importantly, to undertake a quantitative segmentation of British people that would provide us with a national understanding of the pattern of engagement in the public realm.[8]

We asked people a series of questions to do with their attitudes towards engagement, community, public services and politics. We asked them to tell us about the activities that they had undertaken regularly or occasionally in the previous year. These included *passive* activities (e.g. socialising with a neighbour, attending a parents' evening at school, using local facilities, attending a community event, voting in a television programme, visiting a place of worship); *active* engagement involving charity work or the organisation of community events; community-based *engagement* (e.g. engaging in a public consultation, or attending a planning meeting); and *political* activities (e.g. protesting, writing to a newspaper, canvassing for an MP).

Against this we profiled personal time, energy and money budgets. On the basis of factors – groups of questions that respondents answered in similar ways – we were able to create an "engagement segmentation", which we then tested through further qualitative research.

Figure 7
Engaging Britain: a segmentation of the public

Community bystanders	Passive participators	Community conscious	Politically engaged 8%
36%	33%	16%	• Engaged in local politics • More likely to attend community and planning or consultation meetings
• Least engaged across all activities • Less likely to be participating even at a passive level	• Less likely to engaged across all aspects of community and local political life than average • Passive participation in 'easy' activities such as socialising with neighbours and attending school events	• Likely to organise local community activities and take part in voluntary or charity work • More likely to attend a place of worship	**Active protestors** **7%** • Active protestors and most likely to write to a newspaper or MP and canvas for a political party

INCREASING PARTCIPATION AND ENGAGEMENT

© HCHLV 2007   Source: HenleyCentre HeadlightVision Planning for Consumer Change 2007
                                               Source: HCHLV Planning for Consumer Change 2007

The analysis illustrated five key groups with surprisingly clear differences in their profiles and behaviours: Community Bystanders, Passive Participants, the Community Conscious, the Politically Engaged and Active Protestors.

Community Bystanders constitute more than a third of the population. They are the least engaged across all activities. This group includes a disproportionately high number of lower income people, and older people, who are short of energy rather than time. Attitudinally, this group has low levels of "belief" in a sense of community where they live, and the lowest belief in the idea that "quality of life is best delivered through putting the needs of the community before the needs of the individual".[9] They feel disinclined to get involved, socialise or engage locally or nationally.

> I smile and nod but I don't say hello
> Community Bystander, focus group research

Passive Participants also constitute a third of the population. These people engage in some "easy" activities: they socialise with neighbours, they use local leisure facilities, and participate in local school activities. They are disproportionately middle income and disproportionately middle aged. They are heavily skewed towards parents. Passive Participants are typically tired, short of time and energy, and feel unwilling to do more.

> Time spent getting involved is time away from my family
> Passive Participant, focus group research

The *Community Conscious* are a little older than the Passive Participants, although in age profile are remarkably similar to Community Bystanders. But they are much more affluent – they feel time pressure but are not low on energy. They have a very strong belief in the values of community overall, and in a sense of community where they live. This group is disproportionately female. This group – a sixth of the population – make things happen in their community. They organise and volunteer, and are more likely to attend church or a place of worship. They are not, however, "political": our qualitative research did not suggest that they are any more likely to engage in local politics than their less "community focused" neighbours.

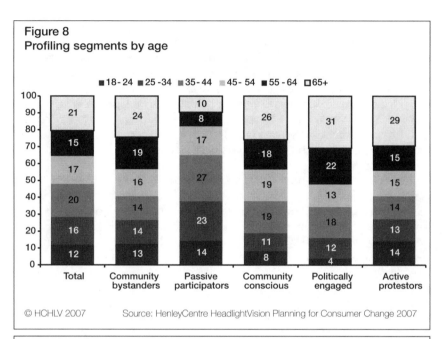

Figure 8
Profiling segments by age

■18-24 ■25-34 ▨35-44 ▨45-54 ■55-64 □65+

© HCHLV 2007   Source: HenleyCentre HeadlightVision Planning for Consumer Change 2007

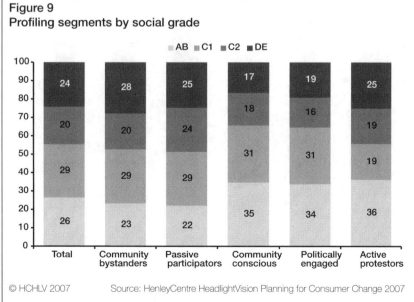

Figure 9
Profiling segments by social grade

▨AB ▨C1 ▨C2 ■DE

© HCHLV 2007   Source: HenleyCentre HeadlightVision Planning for Consumer Change 2007

In profile, the key difference between the *Politically Engaged* and the *Active Protestors* – representing between them the 15% "political" minority – is where they put their political energies. The Politically Engaged focus on local activity – attending local planning meetings and public consultations, and attending or organising other community meetings. They also, but to a much less extent, combine this with "protest" activities: writing to newspapers or MPs, or canvassing for a local political party. The Politically Engaged are the oldest, in profile, of all the segments, and affluent. They are neither particularly short in time or energy. This is quite a male group. They don't spend time socialising with neighbours or going to local leisure facilities.

The Active Protestors are also disproportionately male. They don't socialise with their neighbours but instead put their efforts into "protest" – going on marches and writing letters to newspapers. They are younger in profile than their politically engaged neighbours, and include a higher proportion of lower income people (although this group are likely to be dominated by students).

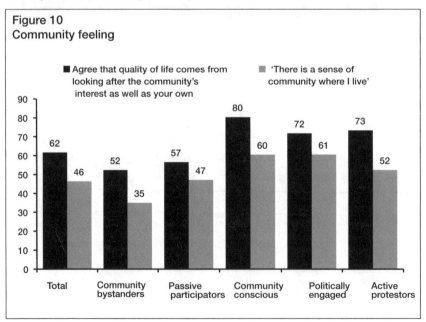

Figure 10
Community feeling

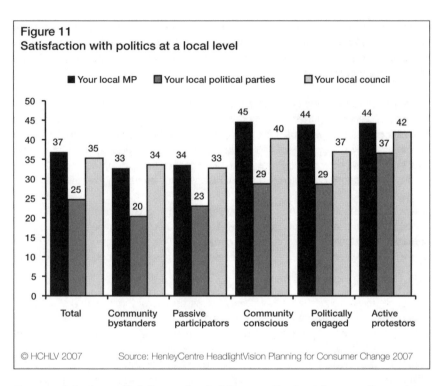

Figure 11
Satisfaction with politics at a local level

■ Your local MP   ▨ Your local political parties   ☐ Your local council

© HCHLV 2007   Source: HenleyCentre HeadlightVision Planning for Consumer Change 2007

Our research shows that those who feel they are the least "engaged" are also – coincidentally or not – the least satisfied with their local MPs, local political parties and local council. They have the lowest belief in the sense of local community where they live and engage least in activities outside of their local area. Active Protestors are also less satisfied than the Community Conscious, and it is probably this that energises them to engage in the way that they do.

This research is still at the preliminary stage and it is too early to make firm assertions about the factors that shape engagement in the public realm. However, the segmentation does shed some light on the complex interplay of engagement, personal "resources" and other attitudinal factors. Time and energy are, without doubt, part of this. The Passive Participants have a "classic" time poor profile – they are focused on working and parenting, and running their homes. They are unlikely to manage much more at present, or at least until their kids are sleeping through the night.

In time, once the kids have gone, they may go on to become Community Bystanders or Community Organisers, depending on their personal attitudes and characteristics.

Without doubt, their socio-economic status has an influence on whether they, as older people, will be vulnerable to the potential isolation of the Bystander – and what may look or feel like a "don't want to" or "too tired to" may actually for some be more illustrative of social marginalisation.

For others, personal preference, personal networks and personal confidence all come into play in determining their level of engagement. The qualitative research suggested that although some Bystanders felt they did not know how to get involved, or felt too shy to join in, or they lacked information about how to engage, the Community Organisers were *energised* by their local interests. For this group, their belief in local community and their desire to be part of it means that they *make* the time.

The Politically Engaged and Active Protestors represent those segments that tend to be known quite well by their local council. They get involved, consult and probably sometimes also pester – they are almost certainly the voices that get heard. This group are highly motivated by their personal interests and have confidence in their ability to articulate them.

The challenge for governance is to harness the energy of those who are politically engaged, while not being dominated by it – ensuring that the voices of others who are active or inactive in the community also come through. There is a need for realism about the propensity for some people – the classically time pressed – to commit time to more activity in the public realm, and therefore a need for focus on the easiest and most time-effective methods for consulting with them. The Bystanders represent a different policy dilemma. Within this group – nearly 40% of the population – are people who don't want to engage or don't know how to engage, or simply can't be bothered. This segment is likely to include those living within the demoralising, energy sapping circumstances of deprivation, as well as those who quite simply, have time but don't consider engaging in their local community, or in "public" life, as a useful way to spend it. This raises more questions than answers and provides a focus for our research in 2008.

Notes

1. For a wider discussion of these trends see Henley Centre and Salvation Army. 2004. *The responsibility gap*.

2. Data from *Planning for consumer change*, the ongoing survey of the values, aspirations and resources of the British population undertaken by Henley Centre HeadlightVision. *Planning for consumer change* is a quantitative and qualitative research programme. The quantitative research is statistically representative across all social groups in Britain and the field research is carried out by BMRB. The qualitative research is undertaken by staff of Henley Centre HeadlightVision.

3. *Planning for consumer change 1997–2007*

4. See David Varney. 2006. *Service transformation: a better service for citizens and businessess, a better deal for taxpayers*. London: HM Revenue & Customs.

5. See www.theiips.com. The Institute for Insight in the Public Services is a joint initiative between Henley Centre HeadlightVision and BMRB. It develops and promotes the use of citizen insight to support the transformation of public service delivery in the UK.

6. Michelle Harrison. 2006. The inequality of everyday life. *Fabian Review* 118, spring:12–14.

7. DCA and Henley Centre HeadlightVision. 2006. *The future of citizenship: a report for the Department for Constitutional Affairs*. London: DCA.

8. The work outlined here is drawn from the first wave of exploratory quantitative research.

9. PCC has tracked this attitude in the British public for more than 20 years. In 1997, 62% of people agreed that the "quality of life in Britain was best improved by focusing on the needs of the community rather than those of the individual".

House rules: making participation mean better representation

By Greg Power

The need to improve levels of participation in the democratic process and find new ways of engaging the public has been a dominant theme in ministerial speeches in the last decade – particularly since the precipitous drop in turnout at the 2001 general election. Yet most of the government's policies address only one end of the equation – the public. Although there is more consultation and opportunity to participate, few initiatives have sought meaningful change of political structures. Ultimately they leave the balance of political power untouched. Yet disengagement with the political process is, at least partly, an indication that the traditional institutions of representative democracy no longer meet the needs of a more demanding citizenry. Genuinely involving the public in the decision-making process requires changes not just to patterns of public engagement, but also to the way in which our political institutions and actors listen and respond.

This chapter argues that public participation is intimately linked to the quality of representative democracy. The chapter examines the extent to which public attitudes to politics have shifted in recent decades, and suggests that although government has recognised the problem, governmental policies have failed to get to grips with the extent of change in the population. Reforms must therefore tackle both public involvement and political power – and the government's failure to recognise this has limited the effectiveness of its policies so far.

Changing patterns of political behaviour

Labour came to power in 1997 promising to do politics differently. Political trust seemed to have hit its nadir in the mid-1990s as revelations about the misdeeds of various Conservative politicians appeared almost weekly. Evidence of Labour's new approach could be seen in the remarkable set of changes to the constitution including devolution to Scotland, Wales and London; a human rights act; freedom of information; partial reform of the House of Lords; and regulating party funding. In addition, the new government placed a far greater emphasis on consultation over government policy, and encouraged use of citizens' juries, deliberative polling and other innovative techniques. More recently, a variety of initiatives have promoted civic activity and citizenship skills, while the "localisation" agenda has sought to find ways of involving the public more directly in the management of public services and delegating power to the lowest possible level.

However, ten years on, politics doesn't feel markedly different. The government's attempts to rejuvenate the political system have included some important and long overdue reforms. But they have not kept pace with the dramatic changes in public attitudes, behaviour and expectations – not just in the political sphere, but socially, economically and culturally.

Several recent analyses have sought to put political participation in the context of this broader change.[1] The decline of industry is often cited as a major factor, and it is possible to track the rise and decline of mass political parties alongside that of mass production, and the large cohesive communities it spawned. It was the collective experience of the workplace, above all else, which shaped the labour movement. And as mass production has declined so the working experience itself has diversified, meaning it is now more likely to differentiate us from colleagues than bring us together. The post-war period has been marked by a decline in collective activity – at work, at leisure and in social life – and an increased emphasis on the individual, as a unit of production and consumption.

The rise of the "atomised citizen" has been matched by the decline of what Pippa Norris has described as "mobilising agencies".[2] Traditional mass-membership organisations such as trade unions, churches and political parties have faded in significance and membership. And with them has gone the familiarity with collective participation and a growing distance with the ultimate collective act of choosing a government during a general election. Other forms of political activity have increased, but these appear to be characterised by individual rather than collective action. The ESRC-funded survey of citizenship highlighted the growth of activity in areas such as ethical consumption, letter-writing, petition-signing and donations to/membership of organisations.[3]

The problem for politics is that the traditional institutions of democracy look out of place. The very idea of delegating representative responsibilities to distant and hierarchical institutions sits oddly in an era that prizes individuality, self-reliance and direct political engagement. The dilemma for policy makers is how to ensure the continued legitimacy of collective decision making in an era of individualism.

Given the scale of change, the political response looks meek. Constitutional changes have been more about updating creaking institutions than changing the pattern of political power. Politics still involves the same actors and institutions behaving in largely the same way as always, but the emphasis on participation, involvement and consultation is a recognition that government cannot behave in the same way as it used to. It needs to find new sources of legitimacy, as the traditional ones evaporate – mostly by trying to improve levels of citizen involvement. But it is a limited form of involvement. And in trying to shape public behaviour without changing the political institutions, they are simply highlighting the extent to which our institutions are no longer suited to the task.

Participation without power?
In this context there are three factors that have limited the effectiveness of the government's policies to promote citizen engagement.

1. Limitating direct engagement
In the first instance the desire to increase citizen influence over local decision making, especially in relation to locally provided services, has seen government edging towards ideas of co-governance. This sort of local involvement has taken a variety of forms, including public representation on boards for local strategic partnerships, New Deal for Communities, Sure Start as well as foundation hospitals and health action zones.

Evidence suggests that there is public enthusiasm for engaging in these sorts of activities, at least initially. However, the extent to which individual members of the public are capable of wielding influence on a board otherwise dominated by professional and political interests is questionable. As Graham Smith notes in his thorough survey of political engagement techniques for the Power inquiry, "In practice citizens are often marginalised on partnership boards – power imbalances tend to favour the interests of institutionalised partners."[4]

This impression of marginal influence runs the risk of increasing cynicism in the long term. The same is true of more elaborate use of consultation to improve engagement. The Labour party's own "Big Conversation" met with initial enthusiasm from those who participated, but this melted quickly as the process appeared to deliver few tangible results.

Consultation and participation exercises need to show results if they are to be trusted by the public. The encouragement of e-petitioning by Downing Street on its website graphically illustrated the problem. It resulted in a huge response against road-pricing, but this received only a muted response from government. The fundamental point is that if you ask people their opinion, you have to be prepared to listen when they say no – or, at the very least, offer an explanation of why those views were not incorporated.

But the traditional structures of democracy are not sophisticated or responsive enough to engage in a genuine debate with the public about policy priorities. And it reinforces the public impression that, as Pattie et al. suggest, ministers are simply "seeking legitimation for their initiatives rather than a dialogue about what should or should not be done in the future".[5]

2. Reaching the hard to reach

Second, ministers have emphasised the importance of reaching the most economically marginalised groups in any efforts to improve participation. There is a general recognition that political participation is largely determined by social and economic well-being. In the 2005 general election 70% of the top social classes (AB) voted, against only 54% from the bottom social classes (DE). Significantly, the gap between the classes is growing. Whereas the difference was 13% in 1997, it was 15% in 2001 and 16% in 2005.[6]

Attitudes to politics tell a similar story. Overall, levels of interest have remained fairly steady for the last 30 years, and according to some measures are now going up. But this masks the fact that interest has declined to below 20% in social groups D and E, but is at almost 70% in classes A and B.[7] Whichever measure of political engagement is chosen there is a clear gap based on education, income and profession. As Charlie Falconer, Lord Chancellor, has put it, there is "a significant minority without a clear voice in and to government. This is a challenge we simply have to meet if people are not to be, in effect, disenfranchised."[8]

The problem is that most of the government's efforts at greater participation rely on people putting themselves forward for involvement, or seek to tap into existing networks and local groups within civil society. By their very nature, therefore, these forms of consultation or local partnerships tend to get at those people who are already engaged in the political process. Influence exists for those who want it, provided they are prepared to seek it out and have the time to pursue it.

Arguably it is the groups at the bottom of society who stand to lose most from the emphasis on greater consultation and participation. Although our democratic structures have weaknesses, they exist to aggregate public opinion and ensure some form of representation and protection for the most vulnerable. The greater the emphasis on direct engagement with the policy-making process, the less impact those sections of society will have. While the better-educated, better-resourced and better-connected are enjoying greater influence, it seems to be at the expense of those who need it most.

3. Identifying the drivers of change

Related to this lack of involvement by the most marginalised groups is a failure to pinpoint the factors that shape political behaviour. Because change in public behaviour occurs slowly, over decades, the factors are wide and various – making specific policy prescriptions difficult. Too often, the rhetoric surrounding initiatives relies on general notions of citizenship, community or good governance. Ultimately, it is an appeal to the citizen's altruism – based on the assumption that the public is as concerned about political engagement as the political classes.

After the 2001 general election the Hansard Society conducted a series of focus groups with non-voters about why they didn't vote. The most telling contribution came from a 19 year old who, after much questioning, commented, "You're talking to me as if I should lie awake at night worrying about this. I don't. And I don't know anyone else who does."

Of course, a concern for the common good is an essential feature of any democracy, but it is rarely the only reason that people become active citizens. What's frequently missed – especially by those on the left – is the role that self-interest plays in motivating political action. The labour movement itself came into being because a section of society believed that their own personal economic and social interests were best served by acting collectively in the political sphere. That social democracy grew in strength was also due to the spread of an "enlightened self-interest" among the middle-classes in the early part of the 20th century. But today the drivers for political action are different – and because our political institutions haven't adapted to these changes, the public have gone elsewhere for fulfilment of those needs.

If the government is serious about engaging the most marginal it needs policies that recognise the importance of appealing to individual self-interest, and connecting it with the process of collective decision making. The much cited example of participatory budgeting in Porto Alegre encouraged the poorest members of society to become involved because it offered the chance of improving their own economic circumstances. But, importantly, it also involved them directly in the institutions of representative democracy in defining public spending priorities.

Combining participation and representation

> At present representative democracy and participatory working are cast in conflicting roles, but both have vital strengths in a strong and healthy society, and there is clearly a need to explore ways in which the civic energy apparent in new participatory working, and the experience of decision-making in the public interest from years of representative democracy, can be brought together.
>
> Involve (2005)[9]

The quotation above captures the problem neatly. Policies to promote participatory activity often work against the structures of representative decision making. At local level especially initiatives have sought to go directly to the public, bypassing traditional representative structures and creating alternatives. The unspoken implication is that this direct form of engagement is in some way more legitimate than mediated forms of representative democracy.

If the efforts at greater participation are to truly engage the public, politics needs to be strengthened at both ends – by shaping public behaviour and changing institutions. Our representative institutions need to become more responsive to public opinion and more reflective in the decision-making process. There is not space here to list all the possible options for reform. Engaging the public requires innovation and experimentation on a number of fronts. Yet there are three obvious areas where new participatory mechanisms could quickly become part of the accepted furniture of representative democracy – specifically in recasting the traditional roles of politicians, parliaments and parties.

In the first place, at the local level the constituency activity of individual MPs offers a base from which to build new forms of representative politics. Constituency work embodies many of the values that people say they want from politics; it is a popular, responsive, non-partisan role which personalises the political process and benefits both MPs and constituents.

MPs already perform a mediating role between local concerns and national institutions, yet there are relatively few means by which MPs can use their constituency expertise at Westminster. This is partly down to reform of parliament – see below – but it is also about developing the role of the MP, and extending the formal routes for feeding their constituents' experience of poor legislation or administration directly into the parliamentary process. But MPs are also hugely important strategic figures within constituencies, providing links with local government, business, civil society and religious groups. Experimentation with new forms of localisation, direct democracy and participatory budgeting needs to draw on, and draw out, this role.

Second, in parliament a greater formal use of consultative mechanisms should directly inform MPs' inquiries, debates and legislative scrutiny. Deliberative mechanisms such as qualitative polling, citizens' juries or focus groups could be a routine part of committee investigations, replacing the rather haphazard approach to research that exists at the moment. Similarly, scrutiny of bills should take into account the opinions of those directly affected by the legislation – based on evidence from the public, and not just on the briefings from lobbyists or civil servants. Recent reforms introduced by Jack Straw have started this process, but they need to be taken further.

Parliament as a whole needs a more deliberative style. In its main debates parliament is currently a place for partisan argument which has little public resonance. Suggestions that MPs should be free from whipping and party discipline are unrealistic, but parliament does need to adapt to a world that is not as familiar with left and right. It needs to be more obviously a place for articulating public concern, becoming more reflective and responsive.

But, third, the most pressing need is for political parties to reinvent themselves so that they move beyond simple conceptions of left and right. Where they were once the vehicle for the pubic expression of politics, their main purpose now appears to be its administration. It's not surprising that the expression of political passion has found routes through other organisations of civil society.

There are signs of change: supporters' networks, a desire to engage with civil movements and more local activity. But for these to be effective, parties need to be willing to decentralise power and control. As yet, they appear unwilling to do so. Such decentralisation would involve a fundamental change, which gave parties porous borders and created shifting alliances at local level with single-issue groups, NGOs and civil society. It would mean that policy making was a genuine dialogue between politicians, members and the public. It would also mean that parties would be composed of networks of people with similar views, rather than members who were exclusively loyal to any particular party.

Conclusion

If people are distancing themselves from the democratic process it suggests there is a problem with the process itself. Yet the underlying implication of most government initiatives is that the problem lies with the public. And policies generally seek to change public behaviour rather than the balance of political power.

Efforts to improve participation must be combined with reforms that adapt representative politics to the needs of an individualised, informed and demanding citizenry. This means that politicians, parliaments and parties must let go. The policy- and decision-making process must move from the current hierarchical deployment of power to one characterised by dialogue, responsiveness and partnership. Incorporating new forms of consultation and engagement into the representative process could offer this opportunity and, crucially, the incentive for people to become more involved.

However, reform needs to offer citizens something tangible. In the long-run the public won't change their behaviour if they think that only politicians stand to benefit.

Notes

1. See Norris, P. 2002. *Democratic phoenix: reinventing political activism*. Cambridge: Cambridge University Press; Zuboff, S. and Maxmin, J. 2003. *The support economy*. London: Penguin and Allen Lane; Castells, M. 2004. *The power of identity*. London: Blackwell.

2. Norris. *Democratic phoenix*.

3. See for example, Pattie, C., Seyd, P. and Whiteley, P. 2004. *Citizenship in Britain: values, participation and democracy*. Cambridge: Cambridge University Press.

4. Smith, G. 2005. *Beyond the ballot, 57 democratic innovations from around the world: a report for the Power inquiry*. Power inquiry, 79.

5. Pattie et al. *Citizenship in Britain*, 278.

6. Rogers, B. 2005. Turnout is really about class. *Guardian*, 14 May.

7. Prime Minister's Strategy Unit. 2004. Trust and engagement in public institutions. Unpublished research paper, 25.

8. Falconer, C. 2004. Democratic engagement. The Constitution Unit annual lecture by the Secretary of State for Constitutional Affairs.

9. Involve. 2005. *Exploring public participation approaches*. Involve working paper 1, 17.

Local government and community engagement: how will the white paper help?

By Cllr Susan Williams and Laurie Waller

> ...too many people still feel that they have little or no influence over the public bodies which effect their everyday lives and that they can play little part in local decision making.
>
> *Strong and prosperous communities*[1]

Local authorities are uniquely placed to understand and respond to the needs and aspirations of their local population and should be at the heart of a vibrant community. However, the inordinate centralisation of power in this country leaves councils continually frustrated by the one-size-fits-all approach of central government. The new prime minister, Gordon Brown, has staked his political reputation on changing the style of central government, promising a new constitutional settlement. But are we really going to see a transfer of powers away from Whitehall departments to local authorities, or is this merely the rhetoric of a politician desperate to shake off a political reputation for central control?

If Gordon Brown is serious about community engagement he will need to go far beyond the meagre reforms outlined in the local government white paper. Essential to the future is local government is the revival of Sir Michael Lyon's *Inquiry into local government*, which was buried by the Treasury on its release.[2] Most importantly, Brown will need to alter radically the culture of Whitehall departments who are currently unwilling to relinquish control over national strategic targets. Forthcoming legislation from the recent planning white paper is further evidence of Whitehall's reliance on quangos as vehicles for delivery and reflects the misguided understanding central government has about the role of local government. If this goes unaddressed it will surely damage the credibility of Brown's agenda and limit his ambitions to empower local authorities.

Local leadership

Community engagement requires strong local leadership and strong leadership can only be enabled if leaders are given the power to deliver local outcomes for their communities, if leadership roles attract the best people into them and if leaders are freed from the target-driven culture that is meaningless to local people. If local authorities can establish strong leadership throughout, they can shape a very exciting future for their boroughs.

The key purpose of Trafford Council is to sustain and improve the quality of life of people who live and work in our boroughs. A newly empowered and revitalized local government could transform public services, drive up efficiency and strengthen local accountability and leadership. By building strong partnerships across the public, private and voluntary sector Trafford will improve access to services and increase public satisfaction, thus promoting public engagement. When people feel that they have influenced what goes on in their communities, this strengthens local democracy and participation.

Unfortunately the failure of this government to reduce the centralising tendencies of Whitehall departments means that effective citizen engagement at the local level is still a distant reality. The white paper focuses on centrally devised targets and processes as a means to greater community engagement rather than addressing the fundamental requirement for strong local leadership: the transfer of power from the centre to local authorities and the communities they serve.

Citizen disengagement
The local government white paper identifies the need "to reduce the amount of top-down control from central government", and to give more control to citizens and communities. It also calls for "effective, accountable and responsive local government". The white paper admits that citizens currently do not feel local government represents their interests: "61% of citizens feel that they have no influence over decisions affecting their local areas. Only 42% of people are satisfied with the performance of their local council."

The white paper attempts, but does not go far enough, to address the problem of citizen engagement and in particular it shies away from local government reform. It fails to propose transferring additional powers which are currently exercised by central government and its quangos – powers that would make a real difference. Government's reluctance to give such powers to councils will make the whole localism agenda far harder to achieve by elected local councillors and promotes feelings of disengagement by the public.

Although there are certain enabling measures within the white paper, such as the introduction of certain by laws and the alteration of the structure of local government and the frequency of its elections, there are few actual requirements within it that might facilitate local participation. For example, the much trumpeted Community Call for Action is a mechanism which already existed before the white paper through petitioning. Its inclusion in the white paper merely serves to formalise the process as opposed to exploring a new avenue for citizen engagement. This typifies the complacent approach of government – its reluctance to address the issues at the heart of the participation debate and to take seriously the devolution of power to local communities.

One of the most widely applauded aspects of the white paper is the acknowledgement that the target culture driven by Whitehall has become completely out of control and leaves little scope for a local approach. In Trafford, the challenge in compiling targets with our local strategic partnership (LSP) for the local area agreement (LAA) was in getting the "best fit" of government target to accommodate local need. If LSPs are to work successfully they must break the culture of deference to central government and be free to build their own capacity. It would be entirely reasonable to allow LSPs to compile their own list of targets, which would then be agreed with central government – this would allow for reasonable checks and balances to be in place while enabling local authorities to take their own initiative in shaping their futures.

Comprehensive performance assessment (CPA) is an example of a central-government-imposed assessment on local authorities, the outcome of which bears no resemblance to local sentiment and satisfaction in many cases. Although many working in local government welcome the development of the new comprehensive area assessment (CAA), due to replace the CPA in 2009, we are concerned about the transparency in the development process and the uncertainty of the outcome. For the CAA to be successful the Audit Commission must recognise the existing constraints on local authorities and the failure of CPA as a measure to aid improvements in public services. At present, there are 1,200 national targets and indicators for a local area. Ruth Kelly, opening the debate on the local government white paper on 26 November 2006, said: "We will cut that figure to 200 indicators with around 35 targets, plus statutory education and child care targets." However, the very implication that over 235 targets and indicators is acceptable is in itself a cause for concern. It is evident from this remark that the government's obsession with a target-driven central command-and-control approach to controlling local government has not ended

Lyons' vision

Very closely linked to the local government white paper was the Lyons inquiry, which was commissioned by Gordon Brown.[3] Not only was this an extremely costly exercise, but the government has yet to begin implementing the vision in it. Lyons has brought into the local government discourse the notion of place making and place shaping as a key responsibility for local government; this is particularly important for city regions such as Greater Manchester.

Sir Michael Lyons' long-awaited final report from his independent inquiry into the future role, function and funding of local government said:

> I believe that local government is an essential part of our system
> of government today. Local government's place-shaping role –

using powers and influence creatively to promote the well-being of a community and its citizens – is crucial to help improve satisfaction and prosperity through greater local choice and flexibility.

In my final report, I call for a new partnership between central and local government. This needs to be based on changes in behaviours from all tiers of government to achieve a stronger relationship – creating a shared ambition for the future. Central government needs to leave more room for local discretion and recognise the value of local choice.[4]

Sir Michael suggests a host of reforms which tackle a complex set of problems, including essential reforms in the short term to tackle the most urgent problems and more radical reform options for future governments.

Short-term recommendations include greater flexibility with less control from the centre by reducing specific and ring-fenced grants, a new power to levy a supplementary business rate in consultation with business, a new power to charge for domestic waste to help manage pressures on council tax, and an end to capping of council tax. In Trafford, the re-localisation of business rates or, as proposed, the introduction of a business rate supplement, would make a massive difference to this authority, which is one of the worst funded metropolitan authorities in the country, yet one of the most economically vibrant in the North West. An end to ring-fenced grants, which are no sooner received than councils have to plan their way out of them, would also free councils from constantly "exit planning" and allow them to get on with the job of providing services.

The planning white paper

Following Lyons' inquiry there has been little evidence to suggest there is a shift in the approach of central government to the localism agenda. If effective community engagement requires stronger local authorities and clearer lines of accountability, then democratically elected local authorities must be allowed the space to deliver local services on their own terms. Local government is too often held accountable for measures forced on it by the national strategic targets set by central government. Accountability can only be meaningful if councils are free to decide how best to meet local needs.

The lack of clear accountability in local service provision acts as a barrier to effective community engagement and damages the credibility of local authorities. The negative public perception of local authorities is skewed in large part because visible increases in council tax are not matched by an equivalent improvement in public services, further reinforcing widely held, but outdated, stereotypes of local government as being an inefficient machine. Furthermore, the squeeze on local government funding in the recent comprehensive spending review (CSR) puts even more pressure on local authorities to deliver efficiency savings while simultaneously trying to avoid the perception that they are cutting services.

There is little doubt that local authorities can meet and even exceed these efficiency targets – just as they exceeded the targets set by Peter Gershon in his review of public sector efficiency – but this could be achieved more effectively if councils had the power to innovate locally. Reforms that rely on quangos for service delivery will only increase the pressure on local authorities and stifle the potential for local innovation. In creating more and more quangos, central government has transferred power away from democratically elected local service providers to centrally appointed bodies, which have confused and inconsistent approaches to governance and accountability. Closely linked with the Lyons inquiry and the local government white paper is the planning white paper, which is heavily influenced by the Treasury's recent Barker review into land use planning.[5] The proposals for a new planning quango undermine Gordon Brown's pledge recently to stop politics becoming a "spectator sport" and pledging to provide a "voice for communities".

Although the planning system needs reform and we need to build more homes, the voice of local communities must be preserved and a democratic, accountable process must be maintained.

> To those who feel Westminster is a distant place and politics simply a spectator sport ... I want to become a voice for communities far beyond ... to build trust in our democracy, we need a more open form of dialogue for citizens and politicians to genuinely debate problems and solutions.
>
> Gordon Brown[6]

The planning quangocrats will effectively be unsackable and unaccountable.

> The Commissioners [of the new quango] would be appointed on a basis that would ensure they had sufficient security of tenure to avoid any risk that their decisions might be influenced by fear of dismissal. We envisage that this might mean appointing them for terms of anywhere up to eight years, and that commissioners could be removed on grounds of misconduct or incapacity but not because of the decisions they took.
>
> *Planning for a Sustainable Future*[7]

Its functions include the ability to "compulsory purchase of land" and "powers to amend, apply or disapply local and public legislation governing infrastructure".[8]

The white paper proposes the abolition of the needs test which currently regulates out-of-town development, and was introduced in 1996 by John Gummer.[9]

Its removal could lead to a new wave of speculative out-of-town development and – in the grocery market – an increase in dominance of the leading supermarkets. Diversity could be lost and low income shoppers would find it even harder to access food locally. Transport-related carbon emissions would rise as more shopping trips would be car based.

The number of people who own their home is now falling. Regional planning red tape and Whitehall targets have snarled up the planning system, while restricting the say of local residents. Ever higher stamp duty and soaring council tax have made it harder for people to get a foot on the first rung of the housing ladder.

Challenges for the future

The need for greater powers to be given to local authorities is now widely acknowledged, but concerted action is need for the "localism" agenda to move from fashionable rhetoric to realisable change. Through strong leadership, local government has the capacity to re-engage a public disaffected by this government's one-size-fits-all, tick box approach to service delivery. Citizens will only be able to shape the communities in which they live when councils are given the powers they need for local accountability to be meaningful.

So the challenge for Gordon Brown must be this: can he bring himself to accept the findings of the Lyons inquiry, which he commissioned, and enable autonomy for councils, provide wide-ranging powers for established city regions such as Greater Manchester, and above all respect the verdict of the voters who are voting across the country for authorities that are not Labour controlled? And how can he square the philosophy of the Lyons inquiry with that in the planning white paper which, while making certain planning processes easier, will leave local people feeling disenfranchised over the larger planning issues that affect their lives?

Although the white paper acknowledges some of the problems of community engagement and participation, it does not go far enough to address them fundamentally. A more radical, visionary set of reforms is needed to allow local government to lead the way in local devolution and to enable local leaders to start to sow the seeds of social transformation.

Notes

1. Department for Communities and Local Government. 2007. *Strong and prosperous communities: the local government white paper*. Vol. 1. London: DCLG.
2. Lyons inquiry. 2007. *Lyons inquiry into local government: final report*. London: Stationery Office.
3. Ibid.
4. Ibid.
5. Barker, Kate. 2006. *Barker review of land use planning*. London: HM Treasury.
6. Gordon Brown. 2007. Speech accepting the nomination as leader of the Labour party, 17 May.
7. Department for Communities and Local Government. 2007. *Planning for a Sustainable Future*. London: HM Government, 92.
8. Ibid., 80.
9. Ibid., 116.

The pressure's on: the lessons from how NGOs engage with the public

By Kirsty McNeill

Democracy isn't designed to favour those who are right but to reward those who manage to be right and popular at the same time. Social movements like Make Poverty History have been able to combine the two, while other elements of the common space have experienced chronic levels of disengagement. The disparity is explained by the ability of the best NGOs to stick to the key lessons that are the subject of this piece:

— Hope sells (but guilt poisons).
— The personal is political.
— Pyramids are built from below.
— Don't beat your opponents, change them.

While Make Poverty History was an impressive driver of public debate and involvement (within six months it enjoyed 88% brand recognition and 20% of Britons claimed to have signed its petition[1]), the colonisation of the public sphere by pressure groups isn't a 2005 phenomenon. From campaigns for women's suffrage and against the transatlantic slave trade to more recent mobilisations against apartheid and to drop the debt, there is a deep British footprint of mass social activism. The formal political sphere and looser social movements were in competition for the public imagination long before the white wristband hit the shops: Gallup polling to coincide with the 1988 Free Nelson Mandela concert revealed that the majority of Britons couldn't name their MP but a staggering 92% of the population knew the name of an activist imprisoned 6,000 miles away in Robben Island.[2] Although the jockeying isn't new, the contested legitimacy experienced by more formal political structures has created a larger vacuum for social movements to fill.

Some analysts have argued that the contest between the two just isn't fair: the simplicity of the NGOs' moral proposition infantilises the audience and leaves formal politics unable to compete with charities which offer principles without compromise or accountability. This reasoning suggests that the public are being misled into thinking that their subscription to single issue campaigns can create a preference bundle unique to them, without the need for a mechanism to aggregate everybody's preferences. The argument contends that social movements demean democracy by allowing people to opt out of confronting the mutual exclusivity of some of their desires (for lower taxes but higher spending, or enhanced civil liberties but complete security), while aggressively disparaging the motives of those policy makers who must try to serve the pragmatic public interest as best they can.

Politics works

This challenge is partly fair: some organisations do present politics as the theatre of sordid compromise, in contrast to the omniscience and moral certainty of "the movement". At its worst, this can tip into what John Lloyd calls a "separation of ideals from any coherent arrangements that might further them ... [they] can't be opposed because to do so is to oppose virtue".[3] Interestingly, the organisations with a default antagonism to the formal political process often have fewer supporters than those that use a context-dependent mix of encouragement and chastisement when dealing with politicians.[4] Those agencies that enjoy the widest public support tend to be those that seek not to replace traditional politics, but to elevate it: while recognising the need for democratic governments to make messy tradeoffs, they try to change the risk calculations by making it harder to bargain away fundamental values during political horse-trading. They mete out political reward and punishment while broadly accepting the division of labour between government generalists and non-governmental specialists. Moreover, some NGOs have been arguably more explicit about the mutual exclusivity of different goods than those they seek to lobby: witness the vicious spat between Shelter and Friends of the Earth about housing supply and the greenbelt[5] or the pioneering work of the environmental agencies trying to motivate behaviour change in a public which feels entitled to both infinite consumption and a world without landfill and climate change.

A further argument suggests that subscription to single issue campaigns is mediated purely by direct debit memberships and quarterly supporters' magazines delivered to the doormat. On this analysis, politics is relegated to an essentially private undertaking, much like joining the local DVD rental shop. Supporters outsource their political advocacy to a professional cadre and opt out of the shared sphere, thereby diminishing the space for collective debate and action. Although some NGO members clearly do view their relationship with their chosen campaigning groups as a clandestine affair, the public's enthusiasm for the white band suggests that the majority want an open sign that they act in communion with others.

In contrast to this atomisation critique, some MPs have expressed frustration that NGOs are far too organised at a local level and undermine traditional party frameworks by organising in parallel to them. But fretting that Make Poverty History created a mass progressive constituency outside parties misses the foundational idea of the whole campaign: politics works. We didn't gather a quarter of a million people in Scotland before the G8 summit in rejection of politics, but to demand more from it. The Edinburgh rally, the Live 8 concerts and the thousands of local events and actions targeted at MPs weren't a negation of democracy but a carnival of its possibilities. The perennial subtext was that progress is possible, governments have the power to create change and ordinary people have the power to make them. By asking supporters to engage with their elected representatives, Make Poverty History orchestrated a year-long rehabilitation of democracy much more potent than many of the "votes in super-markets" silver bullets promoted by pamphleteers.

At their best, NGOs embody a moral clarity and expansiveness that could otherwise be drowned out in the clamour of the public realm. At their worst, they can exemplify a self-selecting, unaccountable elitism that debases our common space. I hope that the following lessons, drawn from my own experience in social movements (but with one foot always firmly in the traditional political sphere), can help illuminate the best of the NGO world for those looking for new models of involvement.

Hope sells (but guilt poisons)
When you sign up to give five pounds a month to Wateraid, you are not immediately told it should have been ten. When you volunteer to give your weekends to Crisis you are not immediately asked to defend hoarding your weekdays to yourself. Smart voluntary sector managers realise that guilt is an exhausting emotion that tips easily into inaction. We know that from our everyday experiences: how often do we fail to phone a friend because we feel bad that we haven't already? Even in instances where guilt does motivate behaviour change it sours our interactions, lacing them with resentment and quiet acrimony. Hope, by contrast, attracts and sustains the best in us. Those movements and organisations that have the most effective recruitment, retention and involvement strategies are those that help people conceptualise a different world and then invite them to be part of building it.

Some have argued that this lesson is inapplicable outside the charitable sphere, claiming that it's very easy to sell hope when talking about saving the planet or ending poverty, but harder to summon inspiring grandeur when talking about recruiting for the council's tenants' forum. In fact, the opposite is true: the bigger the problem, the higher the chances of paralysing anxiety. Make Poverty History asked people to think about an immense global injustice – a child dying, every three seconds, simply because they were too poor to live. When faced with problems of that magnitude, there are two common responses: to believe things can't change or to believe they must. Make Poverty History created a home for everyone drawn to the latter. Selling hope isn't intrinsic to any policy area, but a practice that can be adopted by all who understand that hope is a conscious choice and not an instinctive orientation: "It's not a feeling: it's a decision … You choose hope, not as a naïve wish, but … with your eyes wide open to the reality of the world."[6] Organisations, therefore, can best motivate action by taking supporters on a three-step mental journey: "This situation should change, it can change and I can make it change." There is obviously an interaction between possibility and salience: there are many things that could be made better, and it may be relatively easy to generate hope that change is indeed possible. The next step, therefore, is convincing people that change isn't only achievable, but both worth fighting for and an adventure rather than a burden.

Hope sells best when combined with low barriers to entry. Amid ferocious competition for public attention, organisations need to recruit and reward people for simple actions and that means giving credit for simple behaviour that more active or tribal supporters may consider pretty effortless or marginal. Labour understood this perfectly with its 2001 election poster of an ordinary man with the legend "I did it. I created new jobs for a million people", with a strap-line across the bottom saying "If you voted for change in 1997 – thank you". In a time-poor society, people need to feel that small steps like giving political consent for and paying taxes or turning out to vote can add up to big changes for which they will be thanked and credited.

In this vein, Make Poverty History's offer was, in the first instance, a simple one: send a text message, change the world. Many supporters didn't stop there but the campaign was designed to make this moment of first involvement as positive and accessible as possible. The journey from latent support to registration to activism is a long one – encouraging people to make it means cheering every step they take along the road. Make Poverty History tried to plot over time what we wanted people to know, feel and do, depending on their level of participation. We recognised that if levels of engagement are rungs on a ladder, most people climb from the ground.

Many organisations, by contrast, think if they throw enough bodies at the top rung, eventually somebody will have to cling on. The issue is particularly acute in local political parties. A friend described attending his first ever Labour party meeting as like being mugged: he was immediately guilt-tripped into taking up an officer position he didn't have time for – a classic recipe for resentment, burn out and eventual disappearance. Bermondsey Labour party, by contrast, ended up with 100 volunteers in the 2005 general election campaign after putting volunteer mobilisation in the hands of an experienced voluntary sector leader who escalated people's involvement at a pace they felt comfortable with. Other political parties report similar pockets of effective volunteer mobilisation. The key is hope combined with low barriers to entry and a measured ascent up the ladder of activism.

The personal is political

Many commentators have fretted that modern activism is starting to have "a 'consumer' feel … more of a lifestyle statement than a serious engagement".[7] On this analysis, going on strike or joining a demonstration counts, but attending a concert or wearing a wristband might not. This typography of appropriate transmission mechanisms for political opinion assumes that the harder or less pleasant an action, the nobler and more intellectually substantial it must therefore be. However, it remains unclear *why* the integration of politics into the lifestyle of supporters should of necessity be mutually exclusive with a substantial engagement with the underlying issues. Oxfam now lets you download music from its site, source telephone numbers from its directory enquiries service and even order a wedding dress from its designer stock. That isn't turning the activist into a consumer, it's recognising that the activist is *also* a music fan entangled in a web of relationships and providing them with an integrated political platform instead of forcing their activism to be an alien experience running in parallel to real life. This isn't new, just the latest incarnation of the social–political nexus to be found in an earlier age of Labour working men's clubs or Young Conservative holiday camps. Although there undoubtedly are (and have always been) those whose interest in the policy implications of these semi-politicised activities is limited, it doesn't follow automatically that this is necessarily true for all or even most of the people mobilised in this way.

As the boundaries of our personal and public lives continually change, so too should the definition of what constitutes "political" behaviour. People want easy and novel ways to communicate strength of feeling. Again, this isn't new. The white band of today is the white feather of the last century: the items themselves are largely random but their resonance arises from the political context they inhabit. Chancellor Schroeder threatened resignation after 35,000 Germans posted him their shirts as an anti-tax protest.[8] The extent to which these personal actions became a political common currency largely depends on whether they capture enough of the imagination to become a social epidemic.

This in turn depends on the level of populism in the campaign's DNA. Make Poverty History was able to colonise the public space by assuming that if an idea wasn't as translatable for the *Sun* as for the *Financial Times*, it probably wasn't a sound one. This kind of visionary populism doesn't slavishly respond to public opinion, but instead seeks to shape it, mobilise it and bargain with it. The mass engagement it requires can only happen after pulling down false distinctions between "proper" politics and the kind of multi-layered lives that people are currently leading. Successful involvement strategies recognise that the personal is political.

Pyramids are built from below

Personal politics recognises that ideas are sold retail and not wholesale. To create the political weather you need people to hear about ideas in the most important political forums of all: the local school gate, pub and bus stop. This point basically comes down to levels of ambition: you can attend the debate, or you can infect the water supply. American activist Jim Wallis talks about the most uninspiring politicians licking their fingers and then putting them in the air to sense the public mood; activism that merely focuses on changing electoral outcomes misses the point: "The great practitioners of social change, like ... Luther-King and Gandhi ... understood ... that you don't change a society by merely replacing one wet-fingered politician with another. You change society by changing the wind."[9]

The US conservative movement is a classic example of a group willing painstakingly to change the fabric of their country's politics, town by town, school board by school board. Coastal elites and those inside the Beltway didn't notice it had happened until the movement was so entrenched that it could determine presidential races. Although this was an important by-product of their activities, the electoral cycle didn't control organisational imperatives; instead of going out to win the election, they focused on winning the argument. Their systematic investment in research, communications and organisational capacity over several decades enabled them to frame the conversation and then have it in different ways in different places: at a secular pro-gun meeting in one precinct, but the pro-life evangelical church in another, on a local radio call-in show in one town and the social networking websites of a college campus in another.

Other groups will be able to emulate their success, but only by first recognising that the hard slog of changing social attitudes will happen because people evangelise for ideas – neighbour to neighbour, colleague to colleague. If they are to do that effectively, they must be freed to be creative and tailored and provided with resources that they can adapt to colonise the geographical, social and virtual social spaces that they already inhabit. New technology is helping to create networks of independent change makers operating in a loose non-hierarchical structure but serving common objectives. The power of these tools isn't that they can replace other forms of organising, merely that they can make it easier, cheaper and higher impact for grassroots retailers of ideas to share information and build their own pyramids their own way.

Don't beat them, change them

Howard Dean's campaign team tell an interesting story about the candidate's appearance on crucial current affairs talk-show *Meet the Press*. While conventional political wisdom held that a poor performance on the combative programme spelt disaster, Dean's "defeat" at the hands of an aggressive interviewer produced an interesting result: "First the blog was going crazy … praising [Dean] for slamming [the host] as being inside the Beltway … On normal Sundays we'd be lucky to raise $3,000 [through online donations]. That Sunday, $90,000 poured in."[10]

The media require drama and drama requires conflict. The binary worldview of the talk-show involves an interviewer and interviewee in hand-to-hand intellectual combat. A *Newsnight* roundtable will involve guests with polar opposite views, with the host refereeing over a match in which the object is to win against, rather than win over, the "opponent".

The public, in turn, occupies another mental space entirely. At work, in the family and in our neighbourhoods we value as intelligent and empathetic those who change their minds in response to events, experiences, arguments or illuminating conversations. We need only look to the most popular blockbusters or the holy books of the world's great religions to see that our hunger as narrative animals is best sated by tales of redemption: we like nothing better than a story about somebody changing to become what they once were not.

While formal politics is full of partisans who cite every u-turn as evidence of careerism or duplicity (and some politicians who boast that they've never changed their minds about anything), the most effective social movements know that the big prize is getting people to change enough to forge unexpected alliances. When ultra-right senator Jesse Helms was won over to Bono's efforts to secure increased American development aid, the potency of the bewildering partnership was irresistible to the public and created momentum for a historic upswing in US spending on development. Bill Clinton cited similar unanticipated coalitions – "I know a big tent when I see one" – as the reason he agreed to champion debt cancellation.

There is often a trade off to be made between breadth and depth in coalition building and misapplication of this rule could tip too easily into the kind of compromises that derail momentum. The rule of thumb here is not endless vacillation, but the willingness to encourage and applaud change in your opponents until your own values become what Gordon Brown describes as "the common sense of our age". Unexpected partnerships arrest public attention, but they don't get formed unless people are aiming not to beat their opponents, but to change them.

Churning the ground

Politics isn't the study of who runs the world, but the practice of who changes it. Though not without flaws, vibrant NGOs provide an alternative centre of gravity that rehabilitates democracy by injecting fresh dynamism into its institutions and demanding great achievements from its representatives.

The upswing in public involvement in NGOs and campaigning groups doesn't replace parties or politicians, it just requires them to work harder. Fear of the power of social movements is only for those who, in the words of abolitionist Frederick Douglass, "profess to favour freedom and yet depreciate agitation ... who want crops without ploughing up the ground ...".[11] Make Poverty History churned the ground – others in the public sphere need to start planting.

Notes

1. Omnibus Research HI Europe: sample size 2057, July 2005.
2. Fieldhouse, Roger. 2005. *Anti-apartheid: a history of the movement in Britain*. London: Merlin, 122.
3. Lloyd, John. 2001. *The protest ethic: how the anti-globalisation movement challenges social democracy*. London: Demos, 21.
4. It is interesting to note, for example, that there is a proportional relationship between how "insider" the agencies cited in the piece are prepared to be and the size of the constituency they represent. See http://www.newstatesman.com/200505300004
5. http://society.guardian.co.uk/homelessness/story/0,8150,1393082,00.html
6. Wallis, Jim. 2005. *God's politics: why the American right gets it wrong and the left doesn't get it*. Oxford: Lion, 347.
7. Stoker, Gerry. 2006. *Why politics matters: making democracy work*. New York: Palgrave, 188.
8. As reported on BBC Online on Wednesday, 11 December 2002, 07:08 GMT.
9. Wallis. *God's politics*, 22.
10. Trippi, Joe. 2004. *The revolution will not be televised: democracy, the internet and the overthrow of everything*. New York: Harper Collins, 128.
11. http://www.buildingequality.us/Quotes/Frederick_Douglass.htm

Participation – the role of the voluntary and community sector

By Karl Wilding and Véronique Jochum

Ongoing debates about the state of British society have decidedly moved away from the now clichéd – and discredited – assertion that society per se does not exist, to perhaps more substantive concerns about the lack of participation of individuals in the functioning and governance of the institutions that are integral to a healthy democracy and society. Participation is widely seen as a "good thing" that we would like more of, please, especially if it involves young people or minority communities. Apply liberally, and everything will be fine.

But is it that simple? And what does participation actually mean? Are people referring to political participation or community participation? Are they talking about consultation or participation in decision-making processes? Is it the structures that facilitate and encourage participation that they are interested in or is it the individuals doing the participating? And – most interestingly from our perspective – what's the role for the numerous voluntary organisations and community groups that are both the vehicles and beneficiaries of participation? Whatever the angle, participation is undoubtedly a concept and practice that has captured the imagination and the hopes of many: politicians, policy makers and practitioners from the voluntary and community sector alike.

Participation as active citizenship

For the purpose of this publication – *Participation nation* – we have focused on the concept of active citizenship, a term increasingly used in debates around participation. It is useful in the context of the current article as it suggests that voluntary and community organisations have a complex, multifaceted role in building participation, and that participation itself covers habits and norms beyond the formal or mechanical.

Research by NCVO,[1] exploring the role of the voluntary and community sector in building and promoting active citizenship, identified both opportunities and ambiguities. Participants from a range of organisations, including small volunteer-led community groups and large household name charities, were asked to reflect on their understanding of active citizenship – what it meant to them and what it involved. As might be expected, there was little consensus or clarity of vision of what active citizenship might be. More surprising was participants' scepticism of the term and slight weariness of the way politicians and policy makers were using it. In other words, voluntary and community organisations may not be a short-cut to participation, or at least not to some policy makers' understandings of participation.

Their reflections showed that the political dimension of active citizenship was only one aspect of their conceptualisation. Although the focus of active citizenship has traditionally been the relationship between citizens and the state and the participation of citizens in political processes and governance, this does not adequately represent the sector's role and interest. For participants, active citizenship had two other key inter-connecting dimensions:

— A social dimension, because it was often inseparable from people's desire to make a difference to their lives and the life of their community (whether of interest or of place)
— An individual dimension, because it was based on individual choices and motivations – their interests, their values, their beliefs.

The diversity of the participants' understanding of active citizenship and of its different dimensions was particularly well illustrated when they provided examples of activities that they felt were expressions of active citizenship. Some of these activities were fairly formal – for instance, being a trustee of a charity. Others were, on the contrary, quite informal and far more integrated into people's everyday life – one of the best examples given was the consumer choices made by people inspired by "ethical living" concerns, a phenomenon which has grown spectacularly in recent years. Many activities involved some form of collective action – people getting together around shared values and objectives. However, some were more about individual action, voting for example or, more surprisingly maybe, acts of neighbourliness such as taking the neighbour's dog for a walk.

Of all the activities that were mentioned there was fairly little reference to activities associated with political participation and participation in governance. Activities were more do with community or social participation – or what has been referred to as civil participation. The findings were particularly interesting because they highlighted the need for a broader definition of active citizenship then the one usually favoured by government, which has focused to a great extent on *civic* participation – citizens participating in governance and within state institutions. These findings were echoed by the Power inquiry, which refuted the idea that the general public is increasingly apathetic. The evidence reviewed suggested that although people might not engage in formal politics, large numbers of citizens were engaged in community and voluntary work and single-issue campaigning. The 2005 Citizenship Survey, for instance, shows that formal volunteering has increased in recent years, with 39% of people volunteering in 2001 and 44% in 2005.

A broader conceptualisation of active citizenship might suggest that voluntary and community organisations both drive and benefit from a wide array of behaviours and habits that characterise participation, but that this might not necessarily translate into the dimensions of participation that are perceived to be important by policy makers and politicians.

A policy context rich in opportunities?

Although there are concerns that public policy around participation and active citizenship is too narrow in scope, it is nevertheless clear that the public policy framework supports a significant role for voluntary and community organisations.

One of the three components of the government's civil renewal agenda is active citizenship, along with strengthened communities and partnership in meeting public needs. This agenda, which was initially driven by David Blunkett, cuts across all government departments and is based on ideas that New Labour has sought to promote since it has been in power – governance, partnerships and community engagement. The call for civil renewal is largely motivated by the concern that citizens are increasingly disengaged from the public realm. The key objectives behind the agenda have been primarily to re-engage citizens in decisions that affect their lives and restore trust in political and state institutions, including in the public services delivered by those institutions. As mentioned above, the emphasis has therefore been on *civic* rather than *civil* renewal, despite changes to the machinery of government, which saw the Department for Communities and Local Government take responsibility for the communities and civil renewal functions previously undertaken by the Home Office.

This shift has further strengthened the community governance aspect of the civil renewal agenda: giving communities a greater say in local decision making and in the design and delivery of local services. The local government white paper has taken this forward by encouraging opportunities for devolved neighbourhood governance and stronger local partnerships, with a range of players including voluntary and community organisations. These have been an essential element of the government's vision of strong local communities, active citizens and improved public services. By working more with voluntary and community organisations at the local level, local authorities have sought to improve their understanding of the needs and concerns of communities and to provide services better adapted to those needs and concerns. There is no doubt that the current policy context provides the voluntary and community sector with a wide range of opportunities. However, it has also brought a new set of challenges particularly with regards to the delivery of public services.

The challenges of public service delivery

The desire to change the way services are designed and delivered to better meet people's needs has underpinned government's policy of enabling voluntary and community organisations to play a greater role in service delivery. However, at the same time public service reform has been driven by a market-oriented approach, which has introduced more competition between suppliers in the search for increased cost-efficiency.

The delivery of public services by voluntary and community organisations is not new, but a significant expansion in the service delivery role of the sector in the last decade has occurred with the move towards commissioning and contracting. A concurrent increase in the resources transferred from the statutory to the voluntary and community sector has been evident. The state now accounts for 38.5% of the sector's income, or more than £10.6 billion per annum.[2]

Although measures to make it easier for voluntary and community organisations to deliver public services have been welcomed by the sector, government policies regarding public service delivery have also raised a number of concerns. Mission drift, losing flexibility and innovation due to constraining public service contracts are just a few of the risks that have been identified for those individual voluntary and community organisations delivering public services. Arguments have also been made that professionalisation and bureaucratisation have been the corollary of contracting-led growth, taking voluntary and community organisations further away from the communities they work with.

At a sectoral level, there is real concern that government policies and funding arrangements around public service delivery have put larger and better-resourced organisations at an advantage. The growing gap between organisations with capacity and the smaller organisations that are heavily dependent on voluntary effort is well documented. Evidence indicates that a relatively small number (3,500) of organisations generate over two-thirds of the sector's total income,[3] yet perceptions of a growing sector are building expectations that it can tackle a broader range of issues, including those around participation. The distribution of resources does not preclude this, but it does mean that a finer grained understanding of what parts of the sector can do what, and where, is required.

Co-production and participation

Beyond the polarisation of the sector, there is a concern that government views the sector in a rather instrumentalist way, purely as a deliverer of public services, and that this has been at the expense of supporting and developing the sector's wider role within civil society. It is widely argued that the sector can, and does, make a broader contribution. One of the key messages of our research on active citizenship was that although the delivery of services by voluntary and community organisations is important, other key functions of the sector such as community development, advocacy and campaigning also play a crucial role and contribute to a strong civil society and a healthy democracy.

These different functions including service delivery are not mutually exclusive. The ever popular idea of co-production, promoting the involvement of users in the design, planning and delivery of services, would indicate that they can be complementary. If services are to be based on the needs of citizens and communities, people must have voice to participate in their design and delivery. The sector has a role in making this happen; in particular, it can give voice to people's needs and concerns and give them the skills and support to speak for themselves as individual citizens and collectively as members of communities. Voluntary and community organisations are critical to delivering services that best meet the needs of users by ensuring that a diversity of voices are listened to, providing a link between local communities and decision makers, and by supporting people's participation. Co-production requires engagement with citizens and communities, and this is central to what many voluntary and community organisations do.

The voluntary and community sector – a catalyst for participation
Voluntary and community organisations can be a catalyst for participation in a number of ways. They campaign for change, enable a diversity of views to be expressed, contribute to discussions about the "good society" (the kind of society we want to build) and provide links with decision makers and policy makers. Importantly, as mentioned at the beginning of this chapter they promote associational life and collective action. In doing so, they generate and strengthen social capital, developing a sense of connectedness between people and fostering shared values and norms such as trust and reciprocity.

Through voluntary and community organisations people come together to express their concerns and interests. They will choose to participate for all sorts of reasons – it could be, for instance, the need for support, the love of a hobby, the values they believe in, a sense of community or simply a desire for conviviality, to name but a few. The participation with others itself has value because it contributes to a sense of togetherness – a sense of being part of something that is beyond the individual. It is this sense of togetherness and the social ties emerging from civil participation that are the very fabric of community life and that support social cohesion.

The debate about whether civil participation leads to civic participation is still open. Despite mixed evidence, it would appear that although it is completely erroneous to consider the passage from civil participation to civic participation as systematic, effective civic participation is difficult to achieve without the social connectedness that civil participation stimulates and encourages. This is important, as it suggests that the sorts of associational life that have no clear link with governance or public service delivery are worth nurturing and supporting for their indirect contribution to civil and civic renewal.

Back to fundamentals: active citizens
Voluntary and community organisations provide a space and a wide range of opportunities for people to participate. However, we must not forget that without the active citizens who participate in and promote voluntary action in communities, the contributions of the voluntary and community sector would be greatly diminished. In fact, without engaged citizens much of the voluntary and community sector would struggle to exist. The initiatives and commitment of individuals who come together to change things is what continues to drive the sector forward. This may be through direct participation within organisations, but also through less connected actions such as charitable giving or ethical purchasing. In a time-precious society, the latter are likely to be increasingly important mechanisms by which individuals express the values they believe in and give support to the causes they feel strongly about.

But how much can active citizens do? The increasing and often unrealistic expectations placed on them by government policies around public services and governance is a worrying trend. Are we not in danger of burning out those who are currently involved and discouraging those who are not? The key challenges for those who wish to promote participation is to broaden the pool of active citizens, remove the barriers to participation and increase the ways in which individuals can be supported. Because of their experience, expertise and privileged links with a wide variety of communities (including those that are the most marginalised), voluntary and community organisations can certainly contribute to making this happen.

But it is no easy task. Our consumerist society has altered many aspects of people's lives, including the way people engage and want to engage. Whether they are purchasing a product, using a service or participating people want to exercise individual choice. A key danger is the growing individualisation of participation to the detriment of the more collective forms of participation. Likewise, there is a potential tension between the growth in social enterprise models – where consumers may feel they have "done their bit" by buying ethically – and more engaged modes of participation requiring time and presence.

Conclusion

Collective action is central to civil society and should remain so. However, civil society has also always been about diversity and independence, both of which have been accentuated by individualisation. We should make the most of the wider spectrum of active citizenship, by which people are expressing their engagement and commitment to something that is not just about themselves, to broaden the pool of active citizens.

This increased diversity and independence may make participation more difficult to manage and direct. But then is that what participation is about? Participation has always been messy and unpredictable. If participation is to involve more people, it requires being in tune and understanding what makes them tick – why, when and how they wish to participate. It requires projects, initiatives and organisations to be more flexible and innovative in their approaches to participation so that it is relevant to their lives and accessible to them. Those trying to encourage participation and/or relying on it, including voluntary and community organisations, should work better together to create a range of opportunities for individuals in ways that suit them best, ensuring that pathways are available to them so that they can move from one participation experience to another – whether civil or civic, distant or engaged, individual or collective. Participation matters to voluntary and community organisations, large and small, as such they will continue to be central to debates about how to build participation and, ultimately, a healthy civil society.

Notes

1   Jochum, V., Pratten, B. and Wilding, K. (2005) Civil renewal and active citizenship: a guide to the debate, London: NCVO
2   Reichardt, O., Kane, D. and Wilding, K. (2007) The UK Voluntary Sector Almanac: The State of the Sector 2007, London: NCVO
3   Ibid.

The media and public engagement – friend or foe?

By Nick Jones

Thanks to the increasing dominance of the internet and the enthusiasm with which the traditional news media have embraced interaction with readers, viewers and listeners, there is now an ideal opportunity to match the pioneering work of the early post-war years in promoting what Clem Atlee always hoped would be the people's "conscious and active participation in public affairs".

When it created the welfare state and took vital industries into public ownership, the 1945 Labour government recognised there would have to be a deeper relationship with ordinary citizens and that meant the electorate would need to be told in language they could understand what was being done in their name.

With commendable zeal and idealism, Atlee and his cabinet colleagues did what they could to ensure that the implementation of Labour's programme became a partnership shared between people, parliament and government.

Instead of disbanding the war-time information and propaganda services, the new administration used the existing staff and their expertise to develop the kind of communications machinery that was a first for peace-time Britain but which is now regarded as an everyday tool of modern government.

New institutions and procedures for informing the public began to take shape almost immediately in 1945: the Central Office of Information was established in order to promote government policy and Number 10 started to hold regular daily lobby briefings for political journalists.

In support of the drive to inform and explain, the Atlee government developed an elaborate structure of management and consultative committees on services as diverse as hospitals and National Savings. Representatives were appointed from across the community and most meetings were held in public and open to the press.

Sixty years later the rapid expansion of the internet has provided the state with an unparalleled opportunity to transform both the way information is shared with the public and the whole consultative process. Government departments and public authorities can now communicate instantly not just with the news media but also with pressure groups, campaigners, bloggers and individual citizens.

All these disparate interests can have access to the same information at the same time via websites and email and the resulting sense of empowerment is already reinvigorating debate by encouraging both activists and the general public to take advantage of the many new ways to apply pressure on government, local authorities and big business.

Numerous imaginative initiatives have already been taken:

— Petitions to the prime minister are attracting hundreds of thousands of signatures on the Downing Street website.
— Petitions to parliament could soon be lodged online if the two Houses at Westminster can agree on procedures.
— Increasingly sophisticated forms of interaction have become an essential feature of most current affairs programmes on television and radio and also on newspaper websites.
— Blogs offering factual information and all shades of opinion are multiplying at a dizzying rate.
— Video-sharing and social networking on YouTube and MySpace have brought together people from around the world.

Research suggests that the internet is transforming not only the way information is received but also the way it is digested; two recent studies indicate that blogs are now more trusted than traditional forms of media and that people who look for their news online tend to spend longer reading stories on websites than those who look at the printed versions in newspapers.

What is lacking is any sign of a coordinated response either by the British government or from our wide array of public authorities. So far there seems precious little evidence that officialdom has realised that the internet offers a two-way street for consultation and debate with the public at large and not just the individual citizen.

While many organisations can rightly be commended for the imagination with which they are developing their websites and the speed with which they respond when contacted by members of the public, they seem reluctant to enter into a wider electronic dialogue. Surely, for example, it is time that some of the effort of Britain's vast army of press and information officers was redirected towards monitoring blogs and responding to them.

Whenever I talk to trainee information officers I always ask them if their organisations check what blogs are saying and if they have ever been given official authority to challenge or answer any of the points being raised. So far I have yet to meet a publicly funded organisation which has gone on the offensive in the blogsphere but

I detect among younger employees there is greater enthusiasm for finding new ways to use the internet.

At the root of this inertia is a failure by senior managers and officials to come to terms with the critical question of who should control the flow of information from state to public. Herein lies the key to opening up a new era in communication and consultation.

In almost every area of national and local administration the channels for disseminating information have become corrupted and politicised. At Westminster, cabinet ministers, their advisers and civil servants think nothing of leaking sensitive political information to selected journalists; at a local level councillors and town hall staff are equally culpable in failing to develop new and imaginative procedures for communicating with local residents.

Out-of-date and suspect arrangements for dealing with the news media have become so institutionalised that servants of the state seem to think there is no alternative but to follow the ill-conceived spin routines which so weakened the authority of Tony Blair's government. Hence the Royal Navy's inability to comprehend its own folly in April 2007 by agreeing to let the 15 sailors and marines captured by Iran sell their experiences as exclusive stories.

As the only woman among them, Faye Turney should have been centre stage at the news conference for the freed hostages held at the Royal Marines barracks; her presence would have reinforced the camaraderie of service personnel and the strength and patience of British diplomacy. Instead, by giving leading sailor Turney the go-ahead to arrange an exclusive deal with the *Sun*, the Royal Navy, through its ineptitude, only served to underline the erosion of trust and credibility in the way the state communicates with the public.

What are needed are clear guidelines for civil servants and other officials. They should be told that when they are releasing information to the public they should do their utmost to ensure a level playing field, so that all potential recipients receive the same data at the same time; the relevant codes of conduct should stipulate that servants of the state could not be required by elected politicians to disseminate information exclusively or selectively.

Ensuring equal access would bring immediate gains: all sections of the news media would be on an equal footing and so would pressure groups and the like; campaigners would be able to verify the accuracy of information immediately rather than have to rely on second-hand or perhaps misleading news reports.

By the simple act of seeking to be inclusive rather than selective in the distribution of data, the state could reinvigorate the consultative process. Nothing causes activists greater annoyance than their second-class status when it comes to the release of information.

Additionally, by depriving the news media of the deliberate and often authorised leaks and tip-offs which have become standard practice in Whitehall, there would be no hiding place either for journalists who take advantage of the anonymity of their sources to embellish their reports or for those who have been left out of the loop and who seek to sabotage their colleagues' exclusives with malicious or bogus stories.

A presumption that once the state is ready to divulge information this data should be distributed as widely as possible could help restore parliamentary accountability. A condition of any initiative to widen the dissemination of information could be a requirement that Whitehall departments should revert to the long-standing practice of refusing to speculate or comment on the content of government announcements until after ministerial statements have been made in the House of Commons or Lords.

Moves to restore what the former Speaker, Betty Boothroyd, insisted should be the "primacy of Parliament", might also help drive up editorial standards, especially among political correspondents, because it would reduce the amount of information being supplied to journalists off the record.

Re-writing the rules for Downing Street and the Whitehall departments would be a bold step for a new prime minister because a pivotal moment in the transplantation of the New Labour culture of spin, from opposition to government, was the introduction in 1997 of new procedures for civil service information officers, which gave them the authority to build up media interest in ministerial statements by "trailing the announcements during the previous weekend".

A revised edition of *Press Office best practice* gives advice on how, as the dates approach for the release of white papers and reports, departments should be poised to start a "ring-round" of newsrooms so as to stimulate advance interest and "grab the agenda".

Alastair Campbell, then the Downing Street director of communications, believed this was the only way the Whitehall publicity machine could "raise its game" and get to grips with the task of coordinating and delivering the government's message in an age when the news media were "diversifying and multiplying as never before".

However, Campbell's unseen and unwritten responsibility was the control he exercised over the flow of confidential data to trusted media outlets; he became in effect an all-powerful information trader and like the rest of the political advisers under his command, he demanded that his anonymity should be preserved.

The covert nature of Campbell's dealings with journalists was revealed during cross-examination at the Hutton inquiry into the death of the weapons inspector Dr David Kelly. Campbell acknowledged that he had continued to "talk to editors and senior journalists" despite the prime minister's appointment of two official spokesmen whose duty it was to brief political correspondents at lobby briefings.

At no point during the days that led up to five newspapers identifying Dr Kelly as the source of the BBC's story, did Campbell, in his determination to reveal that Andrew Gilligan's contact had "broken cover", suggest making an announcement in a controlled manner through a lobby briefing, by a notice on the Number 10 website or a statement to the Press Association news agency.

By avoiding official channels of communication and by encouraging his fellow political advisers and government press officers to continue briefing journalists selectively and usually on condition of anonymity, Campbell has done political journalism a great disservice.

So great is the competition for exclusive stories that correspondents have become the eager beneficiaries of the government's largesse in trailing decisions which should have been announced first to parliament. Downing Street's constant push to influence the news agenda for political advantage has resulted in many more unsourced stories quoting un-named insiders, ministerial aides, colleagues, friends and so on.

No wonder political reporting is treated with such cynicism when there is a generation of political journalists who have acquired the freedom to embellish quotations and use them to help manufacture their own exclusive story lines.

Another safeguard which could be introduced as part of any broadening of the flow of information would be a presumption that, when briefing journalists, civil service information officers and other officials should always speak on the record unless there are clear operational reasons against this or other exceptional circumstances.

While journalists will argue that curbing un-attributable briefings will make it harder for them to gain an insight into official thinking, it will mean there will be fewer hiding places for reporters who make it up and the government of the day will also be able to say with greater conviction that unsourced stories should not always be believed and are often pure speculation. Again such a step would help restore faith in the consultative process which has been so undermined by the unprecedented growth in deliberate and pre-emptive leaks.

When politicians hold up their hands in despair and claim they are powerless to act in the face of media pressure, they should be reminded that after repeated allegations of insider trading the City of London cleaned up its act so as to ensure the "full, accurate and timely disclosure" of market sensitive data.

Stock Exchange rules to stop the flow of leaks about bids and profit warnings were strengthened significantly and given the force of law when the Financial Services Authority acquired the power in 2001 to prosecute listed companies for abuses such as the "Friday night drop", which involved holding back information after the end of the week's trading and then leaking it to a Sunday newspaper.

No such sanctions apply at Westminster: there are no disciplinary procedures in the House of Commons to punish ministers who are implicated in the leaking of their own statements. As a result the advance trailing of government announcements, white papers and the contents of countless official documents has become so institutionalised within the culture of Whitehall that the ministers, their advisers and civil servants have become some of the most effective leakers in the land.

If the non-attributable release of sensitive political information about political decisions was subjected to the same kind of rules which now apply in the City of London, then half the cabinet and their spin doctors might have ended up in the dock by now.

Reporters have become willing accomplices, only too eager to exploit confidential information, whether it be an unauthorised disclosure by a genuine whistleblower or a calculated act by a ministerial aide who is quite happy to see a story dressed up as an exclusive in return for some positive coverage.

Given the competitive forces within the news media there is little prospect that journalists will take the initiative and provide readers, viewers and listeners with a more meaningful level of disclosure about their sources of information.

In my view it is the state which has ultimate control over the flow of information to the public and it is the state which should make the first move. If there were some genuine initiatives to embrace the opportunities presented by the internet revolution and if these were accompanied by the introduction of new standards designed to ensure equal access, then the process of consultation could be widened and deepened.

Great strides have already been made by the news media. Television and radio programmes have daily polls on topical questions; viewers and listeners are encouraged to contribute to web diaries, message boards and the like. Such innovations do sound out public opinion and do strengthen the arm of broadcasters when they try to hold government, public authorities and big business to account.

What is required now is some brave new thinking about the procedures through which the state communicates with the citizen; the means are there for a transformation in the way government speaks to nation, what is needed is the political will to match the ground-breaking initiatives of the immediate post-war years.

Part three:
The Public Realm Responds:
Reconnecting with the Public

Participation: a new operating system for public services?

By Sophia Parker

It would be too easy for those of us who have argued for greater participation in public services to think that we have won our battle. Whichever speech or policy document you look at there is a new agenda around greater user empowerment, more citizen participation, and across the design, delivery and governance of public services. From foundation hospital trust boards to the emphasis on engagement and participation in the coming comprehensive spending review, at a glance it seems that government has accepted the principle of greater participation in public services.

However, there is a danger that as the desire for greater involvement becomes mainstreamed through performance management frameworks and better consultation processes, a really deep understanding of what it might mean gets lost. The risk is that the participation agenda becomes instrumentalised, coming to represent little more than a set of "engagement activities" that public servants do in addition to their day job.

I believe that the participation agenda in public services can and should go a lot further than this. Participation could be an entirely new operating system for public services. It could signify a much deeper shift in the relationship between the state and its citizens than the current focus on processes and governance implies. On these terms, we still have a very long way to go.

The real meaning of participation: co-production
The recent emphasis on participation and involvement has bred a host of new initiatives, focusing on enhancing opportunities for people to get involved in decision-making forums (for example, the right to petition in the local government white paper), more innovative approaches to consultation (for example, the development process

for *Our health, our care, our say*[1]), and better use of citizen insight in designing services in the first place (evidenced by a new emphasis on metrics for satisfaction and "customer experience").

These are all examples of opportunities for people to participate more in the shaping of specific services, and in that sense they represent progress. But the participation that really matters is concerned more with outcomes and the creation of public value than it is with existing services. In order to achieve priorities like cohesive communities, climate change and lifelong learning, what goes on beyond formal public services – in our homes, our streets, our relationships, our workplaces – is just as important. There are limits to what government can deliver without people getting involved.

This is hardly a new idea, even if the rather ugly term "co-production" is a relatively recent addition. The acknowledgement that people contribute to the outcomes that public services also support has always been there – see, for example, William Beveridge arguing in 1942 that "social security must be achieved by the co-operation between the state and the individual" – an individual who was situated within self-supporting family and community networks, and where the goal of the state was to "give the fullest possible scope to the free development of the individual".[2]

Although co-production has been always featured one way or another in debates about public services, over the years the emphasis placed on the significance of what we as citizens contribute to the goals of these services has ebbed and flowed. But the pressures and shifts of the last century have served to put citizen participation centre stage once more.

From changing patterns of demand for services, to increased expectations of what the state can do, to a renewed interest in the role of networks and the importance of social capital in making everyday life better, and bringing about positive social change, it is no longer possible to imagine an agenda for public services that does not take account of our role and behaviour as citizens as much as the role of the state. Citizens, professionals and governments need to find new ways of working together to tackle shared challenges, meet outcomes and create public value.

From delivery chains to relationship maps

A recent project we did at Demos on modern family life illustrated the complex network of support that families use to bring up their children.[3] Formal childcare provision was part of a much broader patchwork of support from neighbours and extended family. Of course families recognised the importance of their contribution to the UK through participating in paid work, but they saw the unpaid work of child-rearing as equally valuable to themselves and to wider society – and they expressed frustration that too often the value of this work went unnoticed by a government focused heavily on getting as many people as possible into jobs.

By exploring these families' "relationship maps" rather than the delivery chain of formal family support, we uncovered a host of other players beyond the childminders, nurseries and schools, all of whom had an influence on any one child's life chances; all of these players could potentially be part of achieving the kinds of outcomes public services seek to create. Our argument was not that these informal networks could do a better job than formal public services (although people did seem to prefer them); rather, we argued that the key question is how public services can work *together* with these networks, rather than in isolation from them.

Making participation the new operating system of public services engenders an apparently simple, but profound shift: rather than focusing on individual "consumers" at the end of a long delivery chain stretching from Whitehall to the frontline, people must be understood as interdependent citizens embedded in a wide network of support, including formal public services, as well as a host of less formal interactions and relationships. In other words, a focus on the *interactions between* services and people's lives would replace the current emphasis on the internal workings of services and the delivery chain from provider to passive user.

Part of this shift is about recognising that citizens have more than needs alone: they need to be seen as people who have something to contribute to the outcomes of public services and indeed to the broader goal of public value. Therefore the challenge to government is to find ways of understanding what that contribution might be, and finding ways of encouraging each of us to contribute as much as we can.

But this is not simply about recognising the resources we can all bring to achieving outcomes, important though that is. It is also about seeing the resources we can offer to others. For example, in education, it has been shown that it is parents, not schools, who have the greatest impact on learning outcomes.[4] In care, the value of informal care adds up to £57.4 billion,[5] dwarfing the care provided by formal services, and having a major impact on the quality of people's lives.

Participation as a new operating system of public services would focus on how to enable and encourage greater participation of citizens, not only as service users, but as *co-producers* of outcomes – where participation is as much about offering support, advice and guidance to fellow citizens as it is about making changes to our own behaviour.

Unlocking participation

One of the common arguments against the participation agenda is that it is about government doing less. If the last 30 years of reform have been about contracting out state responsibilities to the market, then isn't participation about contracting out state responsibilities to citizens? Isn't it a new way of putting the old right's argument that an overbearing state risks eroding people's capacity to help themselves?

This misses the point entirely. Although it is true that the participation agenda places a renewed emphasis on the impact of individual behaviour, this is not the same as replacing state action with individual and informal support. Instead, it needs to be understood as a critique of *how* services are currently configured, rather than an objection to their existence in the first place; it is about what government does, rather than how big or small it is. In these terms, participation is about building people's capacity to play an active role – a crucial part of the story while structural inequalities continue to exist. And it is about remodelling public services around people's everyday lives, finding new ways to recognise and strengthen the connections between the host of formal and informal factors that determine outcomes.

So what is wrong with the way in which services are currently organised? What is it that prevents participation from being the operating system that drives provision? Beyond the basic needs of security and welfare, humans seek three things that current models of public services fail to acknowledge.

First, we want a sense of autonomy. The burgeoning literature on self-efficacy underlines the fact that a major factor in bringing about change is our own belief that we have the power to do so.[6] Second, humans thrive on being connected. Despite proclamations that we live in an increasingly individualised society, research into social capital and collective efficacy demonstrates that our degree of connectivity is a major determinant of wellbeing.[7] And third, as Richard Sennett[8] and Edgar Cahn[9] have argued, feeling productive is a basic human need, denied to many and yet with the potential to be transformative. This is reinforced by recent National Consumer Council research that found that "giving something back" was a major reason that people gave for participating, and that this increased the longer someone was participating.[10]

In the current operating system, not only do mainstream public services fail to recognise these essential human needs, but all too often service infrastructures and routines actively work against them. Someone suffering from mental illness is stripped of autonomy, taken out of their everyday life, removed from their networks of friends and family. Dynamics between teachers and pupils, between patients and doctors, are too often characterised by an all-powerful professional and a passive "user".

Making participation the operating system of public services would challenge policy makers to search for a set of reform priorities that sought to build on these basic human needs, rather than ignoring or undermining them. It is through this that new ways might be found to unlock greater participation of the kind that really matters – not sitting around at board meetings or responding to consultations, but being co-producers of positive outcomes. As John Thackara has argued, "Human systems need inputs of human energy to do well."[11]

There are already small-scale examples of participative public services around the UK, which are based on these principles of autonomy, connections and productiveness. Many of them have grown out of "in-between" spaces – they are the result of collaboration between a range of actors in the public, private and voluntary sector, where users and professionals participate as equal partners.

Take, for example, the in-control model of "person-centred planning", which is being pioneered in social care,[12] the growing momentum behind Timebanks, which aims to link people locally to share their time and skills,[13] or Gingerbread's goal to "help families help themselves" through supporting networks of friendship and peer support for parents.[14] Restorative justice programmes, Alcoholics Anonymous and Neighbourhood Watch are older and more familiar examples of what deep participation can look like in practice.

These projects illustrate the impact of focusing on how to address poverty of aspiration and poverty of connections alongside the more traditional emphasis on alleviating material poverty. They demonstrate both the massive potential and the scale of transformation implied by making participation the operating system of services, rather than seeing it as a discrete set of engagement activities that need to be carried out on top of the "business of delivery".

The politics of participative public services
Like other countries, the UK has come to see questions about the future of our public services as technical problems that need solving. If we see participation in these terms, then we will fail to capture the full power of its meaning. Participation is far more than the latest management fad. It is far more than a new tool for reform and improvement. Instead, participation needs to be framed in terms of a renewed understanding of citizenship, and a renegotiation of where power and responsibility lies in society. It is about emancipating people to play an active role in shaping their own lives, and the world around them.

In that sense, participation as co-production goes to the heart of modern politics. It must be seen in the light of long history of democracy and citizenship, rather than a new idea based on the rational, technocratic approach to reform that has characterised the New Labour approach to public services.[15]

Public services are not simply about what they deliver: they are also about what they stand for. They give expression to the values and aspirations of a society. If we are serious about making participation the operating system that underpins our public services, then we need a new political agenda as well – one that raises questions once more about what it is to be a citizen, where power and responsibility should lie, what kind of society we wish to live in.

A new compact between citizens, the state, and professionals

Recent years have seen a new focus on the "customer" in public services. Importing consumer paradigms, where the emphasis is on the customer always being right, and where the goal is providing satisfaction and giving people what they want, jars with the social and moral foundations of why public services exist in the first place. Government should not seek to treat us as consumers with needs to be met, but instead it should seek to work with us all, as potential collaborators and co-producers of social outcomes.

For most of us, professionals are the key intermediaries between our everyday lives and public services. By focusing on the customer alone, consumer models of service risk squeezing out traditional professional agency in the quest for individual empowerment. In contrast, participation as an operating system relies on professionals as absolutely critical players, albeit with a re-cast identity based less on access to expert knowledge, and more focused on building up individual aspirations and working alongside users to unlock potential contributions to devise new solutions.

Ronald Heifetz has argued that the biggest challenge for leaders today is to persuade people that they need to be part of any solutions. And as Demos has argued, we need professionals who view themselves as enablers, rather than experts or fixers – professionals who see their value resting in empathy and dialogue, rather than expertise alone.[16] Programmes focused on workforce remodelling across all public services need to put these qualities at their heart.

But professionals alone cannot carry the burden of participation. An increasing task for politicians in the modern world is to explain to people the challenges involved in tackling complex issues, and the role that each of us could play. To achieve this, we need a more grown up relationship between citizens and the state. Politicians at every level, as well as government more generally, need to recognise their own limitations, at the same time as recognising the strengths of citizens. They need to do this in such a way that they are not simply telling people what to do in order to achieve outcomes, but instead focusing on how to tap into people's own desires for a better life. As I have argued elsewhere, we need a new relationship between citizens and the state, one that is characterised by greater equality, mutuality and respect.[17]

Your money or your time

The emphasis on paid work as the means by which we measure productivity and the health of the economy has served to undermine the value of unpaid work – care, volunteering, community leadership – and too often these things fail to register on the balance sheet, despite the massive contribution they make to the outcomes public services are also trying to support.

Perhaps this is understandable; it does raise one of the toughest political questions of today, which no party has yet truly grappled with: how to recognise the unpaid work that creates public value. This is hardly a new question (just think of the second wave feminist campaigns in the 1970s), but pressures on existing models of public services make it harder to ignore than ever before.

Currently there are two models in play for how to value the unpaid work that contributes to outcomes. The first simply puts a price on it, moving us from a gift economy to a market economy. The model of devolving budgets, for example through direct payments or childcare vouchers, enables people to pay for care that had previously been given freely (for example, by a relative or a friend), if they so desire. For many people, there is some nervousness of going down this route alone, for fear that monetarising that which was previously given freely eats away at the heart of civic life and family roles.

The second model applies to services within and beyond care, and focuses on turning time into a parallel currency – the most familiar, but by no means the only, example being Timebanking. The potential of the internet to unlock new innovations in this area is exponential, as it is a tool that could enable people to group together to make purchases, to trade time or informal support without any other mediating service. Some of the most exciting policy innovations in years to come will emerge from harnessing this potential and aligning it with formal public service provision.

Many of the most successful models of participative public services appear to blend elements of both models: the challenge is not to choose one over the other. The politics of valuing and recognising time and unpaid contributions to public value remains unclear.

For example, we are comfortable with the notion of the state asking us for financial contributions towards public services in order to create value, either indirectly through taxation, or more directly (for example, paying for prescriptions or visits to the dentist). Could we ever conceive of a world in which the state also asks people for their time as another form of contribution? Or a world where doctors are as likely to prescribe volunteering as anti-depressants? Or is the question more about how the state recognises the value of the vast amount of unpaid work already happening, and provides incentives for more of this kind of work to be done?

A possible third option is beginning to emerge, in our homes if not in our politics. The combination of an ageing population, fears about the sustainability of current lifestyles in the face of climate change, and the growing emphasis people place on having time over having money, suggests that the seeds of a new agenda is emerging – where people place as much emphasis on unpaid work and relationships as they do on paid work and consumerism in shaping their identities and defining their priorities. It would take courage to seize this agenda but the opportunity is there.

The answers to these questions are as uncertain as it is certain that the place of unpaid work in society will set the agenda for public services in the future. If participation is to be the new operating system of these services, then it will need to be couched in a wider political debate that recasts the relationship not only between state, professionals and citizens, but also between paid and unpaid work, and the value we accord to each.

True transformation

Without a radical reconfiguration of its basic structure, a welfare state organised around the principles of mass production and functional institutions responsible for delivering services will not be able to maintain itself in the light of future patterns of demand. Across Derek Wanless' review of the health service, Adair Turner's review of the pensions system and Michael Lyons' review of local government, one message is clear: current spending and delivery routines will become unsustainable in a matter of years. Everywhere, the consensus appears to be that improvement is no longer enough in this context: what is needed is transformation.

At its worst, transformation is an empty word, full of aspiration and devoid of real meaning. At its best it is an acknowledgement that the "hidden wiring" – to borrow Peter Hennessey's phrase – of public services needs to change. Taking very pragmatic concerns about the readiness of today's public services to meet tomorrow's challenges, along with the beginnings of an agenda that values and recognises unpaid work as much as paid employment, there is an opportunity for politicians to open up a new kind of conversation about the place of citizen participation in the creation of outcomes and public value.

Deep participation is not easy to translate into a simple list of policy prescriptions or solutions to implement. But when understood as an operating system, it is the basis of a powerful dialogue. With the right degree of ambition, there is an opportunity to reshape public services so that our own contributions as citizens become part of their DNA in the future. The question remains, will our politicians be brave enough to seize this debate?

Notes

1   Department of Health. 2006. *Our health, our care, our say: a new direction for community services. Cm 6737*. Norwich: Stationery Office.

2   Beveridge, William. 1942. *Social insurance and allied services* (The Beveridge Report).

3   Green, H. and Parker, S. 2006. *The other glass ceiling: the domestic politics of parenting*. London: Demos. http://www.demos.co.uk/publications/theotherglassceiling

4   Desforges, C. and Abouchar, A. 2003. *The impact of parental involvement, parental support and family education on pupil achievements and adjustment: a literature review*. London: Department for Education and Skills.

5   Carers UK. 2002. *Without Us?* London: Carers UK.

6   See, for example, Bandura, A. 1997. *Self Efficacy: The Exercise of Control.* New York: Freeman; and Maslow, A. 1943. A Theory of Human Motivation, *Psychological Review* 50 (1943):370-96

7   See, for example, Putnam,R. 2000. *Bowling Alone: The Collapse and Revival of American Community.* New York: Simon & Schuster; and Sampson, R. 2004. Neighborhood and Community: Collective Efficacy and Community Safety. *New Economy* 11:106-113 (2004)

8   Sennett, R. 2006. *The culture of the new capitalism*. London: Yale University Press.

9   Cahn, E. 2004. *No more throw-away people: the co-production imperative*. 2nd edition. Washinton, DC: Esssential.

10 From the NCC "user power" survey. See http://www.ncc.org.uk/publicservices/policy_commission.pdf

11 Thackara, J. 2005. *In the bubble: designing in a complex world*. Cambridge, Mass: MIT Press.

12 http://www.in-control.org.uk/

13 http://www.timebank.org.uk/

14 http://www.gingerbread.org.uk/

15 For more on participation, citizenship and self government see Wainwright, H. 2003. *Reclaim the state: experiments in popular democracy*. London: Verso; and Bentley, T. 2001. *It's democracy stupid*. London: Demos. http://www.demos.co.uk/publications/itsdemocracystupid

16 See Craig, J. 2006. *Production values: futures for professionalism*. London: Demos. http://www.demos.co.uk/publications/productionvalues; and Irwin, A., Jones, K. and Stilgoe, J. 2006. *The Received Wisdom: opening up expert advice*. London: Demos. http://www.demos.co.uk/publications/receivedwisdom

17 Parker, S. The co-production paradox. In Gallagher, N. and Parker, S. eds. 2007. *The collaborative state: how working together can transform public services*. London: Demos. http://www.demos.co.uk/publications/collaborativestatecollection

Experts and navigators: public services in a participatory society

By Dave Prentis

Participation is at the heart of everything that trade unions do. As voluntary organisations we only exist because of the millions of members who sign up to take part, and we depend on the thousands of activists who give time and energy to recruiting, organising and representing them. As democratic associations we are constantly looking for ways of engaging our members and involving them more fully in our policy making and campaigning. UNISON is proud to be a member-led union, with an elected leadership and structures that put lay activists at the heart of our decision making. It's unpredictable and it can get messy, but it's our lifeblood.

Ensuring high levels of member participation can be a challenge as the workforce becomes more diverse, workplaces more dispersed, and working patterns more complex. Many UNISON members work on the move or in remote locations; large numbers work shifts, night-hours or part time; a high proportion have caring responsibilities; some have disabilities or special language needs. Our branches have to find flexible and innovative approaches to draw in new members, many of whom will be cut out, or simply put off, by a traditional routine of meetings and minutes. UNISON has pioneered the use of online organising, "virtual branches" and outreach activities, and we encourage and resource self-organisation for traditionally under-represented groups.

Beyond our own internal workings, trade unions are also a major force for a more participatory society. Historically trade unions played a central role in the social and political changes that extended educational opportunities and democratic rights to the majority of the population. Today research shows that they remain important centres of "social capital" and powerful "schools of democracy", nurturing civic and political capacities that our members take out into the wider community. And in our campaigning and lobbying activities we continue to push for changes that will enable ordinary working people to participate more fully in the life of our nation – such as enhanced opportunities to learn at work, and entitlements to time off work that can be devoted to broader interests and pursuits.

Public servants as agents of empowerment

But in addition to all this, UNISON's 1.3 million members have a special role to play in advancing the cause of wider participation, because as staff and professionals employed across our public services, it is their job to provide the care, the guidance, the settings and the support that we all need to flourish as citizens.

Public services are so fundamental to a democratic society that it's easy to forget how much it depends on them: the education that equips everyone with the knowledge and abilities they need to take part; the medical treatment and care services that can keep us active and able to contribute; the development of local environments in which we can live side by side as neighbours; and the public spaces and community facilities where we come together in shared endeavour. Public services are not just another segment of the labour market or sector of the economy; they are essential for constituting what David Marquand has famously called "the public domain" – a "domain of citizenship, equity and service whose integrity is essential democratic governance and social well-being".

This public domain must be a living and dynamic space, advancing its frontiers to meet the needs of our diverse and changing society. Today UNISON members are at the forefront of that growth, taking public services out to new communities and finding ways to support people at different points in their lives, and extending and deepening our democracy in the process. Child carers in SureStart centres are providing that vital stimulation for early learners and new opportunities for their parents. Careers advisers and others employed in the Connexions service are removing the barriers to learning and progression faced by many young people. Multicultural teams in libraries are playing an essential role in helping members of ethnic minorities access the information they need to take part. Police community support officers and local wardens are making our neighbourhoods feel safer and more cohesive. Home care workers are enabling more people to live independent lives in the community.

Real empowerment of individuals and communities happens on the basis of a series of cooperative working relationships with public service staff and professionals. And as society progresses, these relationships change, too, as those who use public services are enabled to become more active partners in the design and delivery of those services and their outcomes – as "co-producers" or "co-creators" of public value, to use the current jargon.

Of course this has always been fundamental to public services – education and healthcare have always depended on the cooperation and commitment of pupils and patients, and parents and families, to get results. But the very purpose of such services is to give people the capacity to exercise more self-direction in their lives, and for it continually to feed back into their relationship with service providers.

Some of the most exciting innovations on this front are being led by public servants who work with users at greatest risk of exclusion or marginalisation.

For example:

— Social workers developing new citizen-based approaches to supporting
    vulnerable clients through a focus on self-help, campaigning and
    community action
— Modern mental health nursing, which is built on "therapeutic alliances" in
    which those suffering from mental health problems take a proactive role in
    finding their own route to recovery
— Carers developing new models of social care that place user participation at
    the centre of professional practice.

Some have suggested that a new model of public servant is emerging, increasingly
centred on their function as navigators, brokers and advocates, disseminating the
knowledge and skills that people need to take more control and helping them
assemble the package of services they need. It's a role that is continually
developing, but one that will always be there – because as users become more
knowledgeable and better able to access services, new knowledge and new
services are being created and developed. The best public servants have always
been agents of knowledge dissemination and practical empowerment, and that
must be seen as an ongoing task.

Creating the space for collective involvement
In addition to involving users more actively in the process of public services
provision as individuals, public servants are also finding new ways of engaging
people collectively. This is especially important because public services deliver
public goods whose value is shared throughout society, and which we fund out of
taxation as an expression of our collective commitment to common goals and ideals.

UNISON members have always laid great stress on the importance of
accountability in public services, and have been keen to explore new ways of
engaging and involving the public in their development. As a union we believe that
those who use in public services and those who work in them have a shared
interest in making services more effective and responsive. And that the best way
to generate ideas for public service improvement is to create spaces for open and
inclusive dialogue and collaboration between users and staff.

Recently UNISON put that commitment to the text through a unique collaboration
with the National Consumer Council (NCC). We worked together to develop a new
approach to public service improvement called "Shared Solutions", piloted with a
one-day workshop bringing together social housing tenants and staff in Newcastle.
Fifteen tenants were selected to reflect the profile of social housing tenants

nationally, by gender, social class and ethnicity, and were paid a small incentive to cover their expenses for the day. Ten housing officers were given permission by their employer to attend the workshop during working hours. Through a range of facilitated group exercises, tenants and housing officers worked separately and together to explore how the service was operating and how it could be improved.

It was a day of rich discussion and debate, sometimes challenging, but hugely rewarding. Both sides soon realised that tensions and suspicions were built up by bureaucratic procedures that set them against each other and offered little opportunity for a different kind of interaction. As conversations developed, much was learned about how to make the most difference with the available resources, generating an immediate agenda for improvement that was far more sensitive to real needs and possibilities than any top-down initiative or target could have been.

At the end of the day a number of things had been achieved:

— Users and staff had been given an opportunity to build relationships of understanding, trust and respect.
— A wealth of local expertise and experience about what really worked had been revealed on both sides, shared and pooled in a single forum.
— Users and staff had the opportunity to resolve differences and negotiate change through constructive dialogue.
— Local priorities were identified which were tangible, realistic and enthusiastically supported by both groups.

This is certainly a method that could be applied more broadly, and I hope we will see similar initiatives elsewhere. But we know that quality participation can never be guaranteed by the simple reproduction of models and templates. In truth, experiments such as these serve to reconstruct in a formal way the kind of front-line dialogue and cooperation that has always characterised public services at their best. So we need to think about how to create more space and capacity for deliberative interactions like these throughout our public services if we really want to advance the qualitative transformation they make possible.

The future for participatory public services

The key lesson to be learned from all these experiences is that more active user involvement in public services, whether individual or collective, can never substitute for the work of dedicated, skilled and adequately resourced public servants. On the contrary, it is through a dynamic combination of the two that the most exciting results are achieved. If we want to reap the benefits of greater participation, we need to invest in and empower the people who can make it work.

Frontline flexibility and organisational capacity

An elementary point is that public servants will never be able to engage with users and respond adequately to their concerns if they are stretched to the limit by the imperatives of basic day-to-day delivery. Much of the negative rhetoric about public services being designed around the needs of "producers" rather than consumers is in fact a reflection of the fact that tight rationing and cost accounting means that service managers will seek economies of scale through standardised services and rigid procedures. This is the last thing that staff want. But often they have very little say in the matter.

The housing officers in Newcastle spoke of their dismay at being turned into gatekeepers, forced to defend a system they wanted to make better. Many UNISON members experience similar frustrations: nurses who aren't given the opportunity to put their core professional values of sensitivity and patient-centred care into practice; social workers reduced to risk-managing their most difficult cases; and home care workers restricted to 15-minute visits with their clients, with no time to develop the close and supportive relationships that users value most.

Sometimes this is because vital areas of public service, like mental health or social care, remain seriously under-funded. But across the board we see a predominant emphasis on cost control – pursued through short-sighted "efficiency" drives, crude performance targets, artificial market incentives, outsourcing and remote processing. This top-down demand for short-term, measurable outputs restricts the space for the kind of bottom-up involvement and innovation that could lead to long-term qualitative transformation. Empowering users and staff will lead to a more efficient and effective use of public resources, but only if we allow their deliberations to challenge presumptions about the purposes and limits of public provision.

A skilled and sophisticated workforce

As well as giving public servants the time, autonomy and organisational capacity to raise their sights beyond the next performance target or financial year-end, we need to build up the skill set they need to engage an increasingly dispersed, distracted and demanding public. Public engagement and user empowerment are increasingly seen as core skills across the public service workforce, something that is reflected by the Local Government Pay and Workforce Strategy, the NHS Knowledge and Skills Framework, and the government's recent paper on the future social care workforce. One of the most exciting elements of this agenda is the scope for involving users directly in the very process of education and training – something that is well established for social work, for example.

UNISON is helping to drive forward this agenda, developing new educational pathways and increasing access to continuing education and professional development, in part through the work of our union learning representatives. We've consistently argued that employers need to put more money into staff development and offer more flexibility and paid time off for training.

But again we are up against a conflicting imperative to meet short-term financial targets and bear down on labour costs. Last year's Local Government Pay and Workforce Strategy Survey found almost half of local authorities still had skills gaps in customer relationship management and community engagement. In the NHS training budgets and skills funding streams have born the brunt of the financial instability resulting from the government's attempt to create a competitive market in health services. And there are real questions about who will plan and invest in workforce development if the trend towards more privatisation continues. Those services that have gone furthest down this road, such as home care, are suffering the effects of a largely deregulated and increasingly casualised workforce.

Integrated services, embedded in communities
If public services are to constitute a truly public realm, they must be properly interconnected and genuinely open to the public. Public servants need to become practised in partnership working, keeping up with developments across organisational and professional boundaries, so they can guide users to the services that they need.

This means finding ways to repair the fragmentation and dislocation that characterises large parts of our public service landscape. Increasingly we are finding that the price of competition and contestability is the loss of coordination and continuity. A key issue for social tenants and housing officers in Newcastle was the organisational complexity resulting from the transfer of stock to an arms-length management organisation. In health and social services the incentives to chase income and externalise costs are making it harder for professionals and their patients to find the right care pathways. And the requirement on schools and hospitals to compete for mobile families and patients can work against attempts to strengthen local accountability and involvement.

Some see the incorporation of the "third sector" and "social enterprise" into service delivery as part of the solution. UNISON has always celebrated the contribution of community and voluntary organisations to advancing social justice and active democracy. Many of our members work in them. But like others in the sector, we are concerned that their special relationship with user communities will be weakened if they are drawn into a competition for contracts, squeezing their scope for advocacy and social innovation. Developing a more participatory public sector will remain the central challenge, and we need to find ways of working with and learning from community and voluntary organisations that supports their unique role as independent sources of ideas and energy.

Conclusion

Increased public participation can throw up challenges and tensions, but it also offers the best means of resolving them constructively and creatively. In our public services, a more participatory approach, combining the capabilities and commitment of users and staff, could offer an alternative to the top-down imposition of targets and markets that have done so much damage to the fabric of our public domain.

But this will mean there must be a commitment of resources over the long term, and a readiness to rethink the rationale of public service "reform". Otherwise the danger is that a rhetoric of participation will be superimposed on a harsh reality of crude cost control. If "user empowerment" is seen as a substitute for workforce investment, or as a device for legitimating cuts in service provision, it will only breed cynicism and disaffection on all sides. The test will be whether the government is prepared to let participatory alliances between users and staff create new pressures for better public services.

Politics and political engagement: for the public good?

By Rt Hon Douglas Alexander MP

In a country where a recent poll showed MPs are less trusted than used car salesmen,[1] it can seem foolhardy to argue that our greatest challenge is to renew and not to replace politics. I state this not just as a practising politician but also as a citizen and parent. We now live in a world where the challenges we face, whether environmental, social or economic, are beyond the remit of bureaucratic institutions or markets alone. To tackle these issues and leave a legacy of progressive and sustainable social change each of us must take responsibility for action. Be it on climate change, persistent inequality and poverty or terrorism, only as individuals and communities working together will we be able to resolve these problems in a way that benefits us all. To make such collaboration possible we need forums in which we can come together to decide how to act and how to best use the limited resources at our disposal. That the public are turning away from party politics isn't simply a problem for politicians in justifying their existence. It challenges our very capacity as a society to act to address the problems that will affect all our lives and those of future generations. Put simply, in the uncertainty of the modern world, politics is the best chance we as a society have of finding shared solutions to our shared problems.

Concern about declining public engagement in politics is widespread and non-partisan. The difficulties are not just evident in falling turnout in elections or trust in politicians. The annual Electoral Commission and Hansard Society Audit of Political Engagement throws the challenge we face into sharp relief. It shows that the public remain as opinionated and passionate about the condition of their country as previous generations; they care about "political" issues. Yet in the past three years, a time period that included a general election, only two out of five people state they have discussed "politics" with someone else. As the Audit states this reveals the public "fail to associate the word 'politics' with issues that affect their everyday lives".[2] The problem facing those of us who care about the condition of our democracy is not that the public are angry or disillusioned with contemporary politicians. It is instead the relentless trend of marginalising politics altogether as part and parcel of British life.

As others in this pamphlet have described, we are also a nation where political parties face competition not only from each other, but from many other directions in securing the time, interest and energy of the public. Voting, volunteering or organising for good causes are all acts that fuel democratic debate and activity. Inevitably the public's capacity to do these things is constrained by the obligations of everyday life. However, just as politicians seek to engage people in their work, so too others in corporate, social and voluntary organisations also compete to secure their attention and activism – and are increasingly winning. It is not simply these alternative activities that are challenging political parties; they are ever more positioned as the real way in which social change occurs. Consider the comments of designer Anya Hindmarch referring to the campaign to replace plastic bags in supermarkets with reusable ones.

> I think there is a mistrust of politicians, and probably businesses and fashion and other aspects of society can influence in a more powerful and direct way.[3]

The participation of "non-political" actors in public policy is not a new phenomenon. Be it through commenting, lobbying or campaigning, businesses, charities and pressure groups have always engaged in public life. What is new is how the public are substituting, not supplementing, social and consumer activism for political participation. We are now a nation where the public often choose to act on their views not through political campaigning or the ballot box, but ever more through their personal consumption patterns, community activism or challenging corporate and social entities.

These organisations are also often better at engaging people in a format that fits with real life, seeking incremental rather than total commitment to their cause and encouraging all forms of participation in their work. Where political parties start by demanding membership, meeting attendance and leaflet rounds, charities such as Oxfam begin by asking supporters to donate, change their purchasing power or simply send an email. This is not just about national politics. At a local level, too, community and voluntary campaign groups are often more flexible in their structures, enabling members to balance childcare and work commitments with activism or using modern technology to connect with time pressed citizens. Starkly different to the evidence of falling participation in the public realm, the impact of this shift is clear across society – whether in the 40% of Britons give voluntary help to a charity,[4] the 18% of the population who boycott goods for ethical reasons[5] or the two and half million supporters of Cancer Research participating in their healthcare campaigns. As levels of political activism have declined so these "non-political" endeavours have flourished.

Detachment by the public from politics and growing interest in social and consumer campaigning changes the very terms of debate about the role of politics – and politicians – in our daily lives. Too often in discussion about democracy there is a presumption that the public will make time for politics and the problem is procedural or personal. Innovations such as postal voting, mobile polling stations and e-ballots have helped to boost turnout, but in themselves they do not overcome the growing gap between the British public and their political representatives. This is because voting is, and will remain, an intensely political act and should be valued as such. The causes for this detachment lie deeper in British society than just the difficulty of getting to polling stations on a workday or a dislike for today's MPs.

So how should we respond? Not to be feared, we should welcome a public realm with so many differing actors as an opportunity for greater debate and discussion. Democratic voice can and should be exercised in many ways in an open society – but we should be clear that alone it is not enough to find shared solutions to shared problems. That is the job of politics. Indeed, in a modern age where so many new and old voices call for action on a multitude of topics it is a job that grows in its importance, not diminishes.

But to make progress, we need to renew our sense of the value of this job to our everyday lives and our shared concerns – and the difference between this and the role that non-political organisations play in our society. First, politics and democracy requires a concern for equality of participation. Social campaign groups or corporate actors do not claim to represent the needs of society as a whole. They segment the public, seeking the support of those who can shout the loudest or be most influential in promoting their interests. In contrast the legitimacy of our democratic institutions rests on being forums in which all citizens can give voice and vote to their views. So too, a political movement thrives by being broad based and capable of gaining support from not just those with authority but across all sections of society.

Second, politics is a necessarily collective endeavour, which seeks action not on one issue but across a range of social and economic concerns. Consequently it requires us to think not just as "I" the taxpayer but also "we" the community. Although a single issue group can accommodate people who diverge on other topics by focusing on a specific concern, a political party seeks to act across a range of areas of concern so it needs a shared vision of how the world could be to bring its members together. Ideology allows members of a political party to broker the necessary compromises that mean they can work together for the long term – not just agree momentarily issue by issue.

This reflects how politics is as much about decision making as it is about debate. It is the capacity of engagement in political processes to determine outcomes that separates it from pure discussion. So political parties have to be able to act as well as lobby. They are not single issue pressure groups, but broad coalitions designed to enable political ideals to be put into practical programmes for change which secure a mandate at the ballot box. Finally, and above all, democracy is a forum also defined by tough questions of accountability. These are the checks and balances that ensure that it is able to meet the first three requirements. Supporters may withdraw their donations if they disagree with the leadership of a campaign, but there is little expectation that the head of Greenpeace will be answerable to members in the same way parties hold MPs and ministers to account.

A thriving democracy needs both those who advocate a cause with single-minded vigour and those who are willing to decide between competing demands in order to frame a programme for government. This is not simply a point of political philosophy. We see in our contemporary society how when social concerns are given political leadership, joint action can be a force for good in a troubled world. The public engagement in international debt through the Make Poverty History campaign helped to deliver more progress in tackling poverty than political debate alone could achieve. Yet this was only possible because the politicians responsible for balancing the demands made with the needs of governance shared the objectives of the endeavour. Progressive campaigning that engaged the public helped to speed the pace of political change; with common cause they worked together.

To recognise how the two can work together is not to suggest they cannot clash or that government should prioritise populism over political principles. Rather it is to recognise that both are valuable to our democratic process because they each play a different role in raising concerns and securing action on them. As a result our debates and our decision making are diminished if political parties simply become vehicles for single-issue pressure groups or this week's public opinion poll – or if NGOs and charities exert influence without being held accountable for the positions they espouse.

Yet if we get the job of politics right, we must not forget the practicalities. Whether in local or national forms of governance political parties can learn organisational lessons from outside politics. In particular, many of the most successful social campaigns were rooted in encouraging activism organically rather than through rigid structures. The Make Poverty History campaign set a broad national framework of objectives, but was driven on the ground by a coalition of groups who each had a different angle on the debate. Thus some people were first drawn in as members of Christian Aid, others through the fair-trade movement and others from Jubilee 2000. Instead of trying to restrict each of these groups to one set of topics, Make Poverty History encouraged them to talk about the matters they were primarily interested in and then use this as a springboard to raise other aspects of the campaign. Activists on the ground then reached out to people using their local knowledge and personal passion for a subject to bring energy and enthusiasm to their work.

This is also the case in my own party where it is not formal structures but local innovation which is leading the way in reconnecting the public with their political representatives. Examples range from members in Newcastle using the social networking technology of Facebook to coordinate campaigning activity, activists in Walthamstow organising community consultations on how to tackle local child poverty and councillors in Southwark and Bermondsey using a volunteer coordinator to help use the time people have to give to politics to best advantage. Each very different, each illustrating how political parties can capture the public's imagination by drawing on the talents and interests of their strongest asset – the people who are their members.

Sometimes these questions of political process or party renewal are seen as incidental to the bigger problems of policy concerns; that they are the preserve of political apparatchiks who value standing orders over substantive matters. Others argue we need politics because, as Churchill once quipped, "Democracy is the worst form of government except all the others that have been tried." Such cynicism about politics has always been part of the British democratic psyche as well as a healthy demand for dissent against those seen as authority figures and our discussions would be poorer without it. So too we cannot pretend renewal of political engagement is easy or somehow simple. Because it requires making and upholding difficult decisions, politics is inevitably always less enticing as a pursuit than single issue campaigning. We must also recognise concern about the conduct of politicians must not be ignored or considered unmerited. It will always be easier to admit to being a member of Greenpeace than to being a political activist or even a politician, however much we say we value the political institutions of our society.

Yet I believe the need to renew the role of politics goes beyond reaffirming the importance of our democratic heritage or legitimising decision making. It is its unique capacity to create opportunities for common endeavour that shows how it is the best chance we have to tackle the policy challenges we will face in the years ahead. And in leading those debates and addressing those concerns, it is politicians who are a group uniquely equipped to bridge the gap between citizens and government. Whether in tapping into the expertise of public service workers, encouraging active citizenship or promoting corporate social responsibility, politicians can play a vital role in helping every actor in the public realm to work together. And we know from other chapters in this book the value of such collaboration and cooperation. Whether in empowering children to learn in ways that help them flourish, or in generating a consensus on our mutual obligation to tackle climate change, the benefits to working together far exceed the difficulties. Any politician will tell you they cannot change the world alone. However, by enabling the public to debate, discuss and decide the way forward it is politics which offers us the best chance to do so together.

The tectonic plates that once defined the British public realm continue to shift. As this pamphlet reveals, the attention and interest of citizens is a commodity political institutions can no longer take for granted, and rightly so. The challenge for every one of us who acts in the public realm is to respond to these changes in ways that uphold the vital role that politics and political parties play alongside social, corporate and charitable organisations in determining our future. The people of Britain need and deserve nothing less.

Notes

1   Readers Digest Poll on 8 May 2007. http://uk.news.yahoo.com/afp/20070508/tpl-britain-politics-offbeat-5b839a9.html

2   Hansard Society. 2007. *Audit of Political Engagement 4*. London: Hansard Society.

3   "I'm no hypocrite" insists Anya Hindmarch. *Daily Mail*. 7 May 2007.

4   Ipsos MORI, September 2005. Atkinson Simon Presentation, Involve seminar. 21 May 2007.

5   Ibid.

Critical mass: broadening the reach of public engagement across society

By Richard Wilson and Alice Casey

Politics is about to get difficult. Academics at institutions as wide ranging and esteemed as the Kennedy School of Government,[1] the LSE,[2] OECD[3] and beyond, all agree that national politics will for the foreseeable future be dominated by the "wicked" issues.[4] The pollster MORI suggests that such wicked policy challenges will come to characterise British national politics over the next few years.[5] According to its director Ben Page: "We are entering a period where all the easy political wins have been made."[6]

At the same time as the rise to prominence of the wicked policy problems, there is greater attention being given to the need to engage the public. Both Brown[7] and Cameron[8] are promising us a New Politics, a kind of politics which will be more citizen centred. Calls for greater engagement have been escalating ever since the 2001 election and recently reached boiling point in Brown's first speech as prime minister.[9]

These two phenomena are not unrelated. It has become clear to many in policy circles that in order to introduce the measures required to address the tough issues we face, public understanding of the issues and support for the policy responses is required. Not just because this understanding and support helps when delivering potentially controversial legislation, but because the limits of "government-as-usual" are becoming clear. After all, how can we *force* people to use energy in their homes responsibly? Or eat healthily? Or save for their retirement? Yes, government can play a role but results also require actions and behavioural change from individuals. For decades many at the heart of government have believed that the policies needed to address wicked issues are electoraly untenable. It is assumed that there are no votes in fuel taxes, dieticians and pension contributions.

Yet when you speak to politicians of all persuasions off the record on such issues, they often agree that these are the kind of policy responses most likely to take us towards reaching shared goals of tackling climate change, obesity or increased saving for retirement.[10]

It is no coincidence that in the last two years the government has commissioned four large citizens' jury[11] style events on health care (Your Health Your Care Your Say), pensions reform, climate change and nuclear power. Four wicked issues if ever there ever were any.

Evaluations of these processes have demonstrated clear success in terms of creating valuable information for decision makers in the form of social research data (e.g. public opinion information) and significantly improved the quality of traditional consulting techniques, as well as creating new forums for politicians and citizens to interact meaningfully.[12]

We also have evidence from recent research that these national public engagement processes do effectively engage citizens constructively in wicked policy issues and support considered responses.[13] These processes also can help build people's capacity to become active citizens; significantly improve policy; create more transparent government; build social capital; and encourage people to become more engaged in formal politics.

Distributing the benefits
There are two key challenges, however: first and most critically that of scale. We know that the key benefit of engagement, necessary for progress on the wicked issue, is only ever gained by those citizens who get directly involved in the deliberative events.

GM Nation, the UK's biggest ever official public engagement process, engaged 20,000 people directly in events.[14] The National Pensions Debate and Your Health Your Care Your Say (YHYCYS) directly involved 1,075[15] and 1,240[16] people, respectively. Each of these initiatives also used surveys and other communication tools to engage more citizens, but these indirect mechanisms do not support the deliberation required for deep engagement with tough issues.

YHYCYS and GM Nation achieved reasonable levels of public awareness (18% and 28%, respectively). However, awareness is not the same as genuine engagement in the issues. Engagement is what we need. Without widespread engagement it is impossible to build a critical mass of support for the tough policy issues we face. In short we need to go from engaging a few thousand people to engaging millions of people.[17]

Broadcast media and conflict
Cue the broadcasters. Shouldn't they be doing this? Don't they after all have the reach? Don't they have public service remits? Well maybe. It depends how you interpret their objectives.

The obvious candidate is the BBC, which was re-chartered last year with six new public purposes, the first of which is "Sustaining citizenship and civil society". There is a vociferous debate inside and outside the BBC at present[18] around how to interpret this public purpose. One of the key challenges is a tension between traditional journalists and the need to engage people in important issues.[19] A prerequisite for media coverage is often conflict, especially in news and current affairs. The culture of news journalism in the UK is founded on positional debate, we hear it each morning on the *Today* programme and see it before we sleep on *Newsnight*. Many of the issues that require public engagement are not as conflict ridden as others and therefore by definition not as newsworthy.

This explains to an extent why there has been very limited media take up of these citizens' juries as newsworthy content. Mark Easton, the BBC Home Affairs editor, filmed "The Health Debate" and "The No 10 Policy Review" for BBC news, and found that: "at present it is extremely difficult to translate these processes into engaging content".

Peter Bazalgette, ex-chair of Endemol, the makers of *Big Brother* and board member of YouGov, suggests "we need to move away from presenting current affairs as worthy and intellectual, and instead present information in a way that it connects to people's emotions in a way that excites them".

So, with the current state of affairs we as a society don't engage with many of these crucial issues as they either do not fit the requirements that govern our national broadcast slots; or we the viewing public simply find them too dull.

Beyond deliberative research

The second challenge we face is that much of the national level public engagement undertaken in the UK is not strictly public engagement, but deliberative research. This may sound like an academic point, but its significance became clear to me in the summer of this year when I observed one of the world's biggest ever public engagement processes CaliforniaSpeaks. It was led by the Governor Arnold Schwarzenegger and delivered by US democratic pioneers AmericaSpeaks, whose model of engagement was used as the basis for Brown's citizens' juries. The principal difference, however, is that in the UK these juries are run as exercises in deliberative research to inform decision makers, whereas in the USA they are first and foremost platforms for citizen voice. This is an understandable manifestation of the UK and US contexts. In the USA there is only patchy institutional support for such activities, the drivers have come from the bottom up, methods are developed by democratic campaigners and funded by charitable trusts.

In the UK by contrast most of the high profile national public engagement activities have been funded by public institutions, and been delivered by social and opinion research agencies. Consequently our national public engagement processes are top down initiatives to provide decision makers with deliberative opinion research. In the USA their processes give greater attention to citizens' needs, such as helping them take their views forward after the event, and providing ongoing feedback as to how their contributions have made an impact. In the UK we have much greater opportunities for genuine influence and the processes are often very thorough. To really ensure the investment in these processes leads to long-term citizen engagement, however, we in the UK need to ensure that our processes are more responsive to citizens' needs.

Where next?
So where does that leave us? Well we are world beaters at national deliberative research events. We also have the worlds most respected and trusted national broadcaster with newly established citizenship commitments. We probably have as much institutional support for public engagement as any nation on earth and a prime minister and cabinet explicitly committed to creating a newly engaged citizenry. This is a good place to be.

Going beyond the room – engaging millions
Our first step is going beyond the room to make our "national" public engagement processes *truly* national by engaging millions not thousands in the discussions. To make this work we need to look at where we are successfully engaging millions of people already. National voting mechanisms that are perceived to connect to real power do engage millions of us, whether they are the national elections or Number 10's e-petitions. Voting-based TV shows such as *X-Factor* and *Big Brother* have created a phenomenon both in engaging citizens but also in generating revenue; they have changed the face of our television and it is time that we translated the lessons that Endemol and others can offer into the political realm. Another avenue that is engaging millions of people are the social networking sites of Facebook and Myspace. The 30 million users of the Facebook social networking site are driving innovation in public engagement at an exponential rate; for many it has already overtaken email as the communication method of choice and through 3G mobile phones is becoming an integral part of their lifestyle.

Not all routes to millions of people are dominated by dissemination pathways of traditional or new media. Perhaps the most interesting element of the Californian mass engagement initiative was a smaller community session that was run in a library and linked to the high profile events using a basic webcam. The citizens who attended the local library event were able to engage with all the materials online just as people were who attended the large events, and were able to vote online. The participants are reported to have appreciated the convenience of being in their own community but still felt that essential connectivity to a larger and significant process.

Another route to widespread engagement which would support the community deliberations are DIY engagement kits. We in the UK have developed a strong track record in developing products and games designed to help people engage with issues. We should take the best of these and present them beautifully and accessibly to ensure they are as user friendly as possible.

One of the problems with our existing DIY engagement kits is that they have usually operated in isolation from larger policy processes or media campaigns. If we are going to go down the DIY approach it is essential we learn from California Speaks and ensure those community participants are connected to the larger, high profile process.

From deliberative research to public engagement

Our second step is moving from national deliberative research to national deliberative public engagement. Involve is currently working with the National Consumer Council (NCC) to develop a code on deliberative public engagement, which should help. The code will emphasise the need to pay close attention to citizens as well as the institutions. The code is currently in development but particular emphasis is likely to include supporting citizens to have voice after the events and ensuring the information used to support engagement is presented independently. These are small changes but are required to make the step from research to engagement.

New political leadership

Our third and final step relates to political leadership. The recent controversy over the nuclear consultation has highlighted the challenge of having traditional political leadership running alongside attempts to engage the public. Traditionally politicians set out clear visions for the public to choose to buy into or not. The more specific the vision the better, as the more accountable the politician who outlines the vision will be to the fulfilment of their promises. The problem with traditional specific political visions is that by their very nature they close down the options for public debate and engagement. If a prime minister says "I want the UK to continue using nuclear power" it is extremely problematic to have an open deliberative process on whether nuclear power is a good idea. New Politics and public engagement requires politicians to set more open visions on their priorities, which support debate by the many and not the few.

Practical options

It seems therefore that we are at a critical stage when the parts of a really effective national public engagement initiative are available to us, and what we need to do is to bring them together to create a whole immeasurably bigger than the sum of the parts. So how might a national public engagement process that engaged a critical mass of citizens in a tough policy issue actually look? In going forward there are seven overarching lessons. Whatever we do must be:

— **Citizen centred:** We must design what we do around the citizens we seek to engage. Too often processes are developed from the perspective of institutions.
— **Deliberative:** Whatever we do next must involve deliberation. This is something we already do well and is proven to support the necessary deeper engagement.
— **Highly engaging:** Our aim must be to ensure our processes are such a delight to be part of that we are overwhelmed by demand to take part. Such demand would be a true measure of success. The process must have this goal at heart.
— **Connected to policy:** There must be an understandable connection to real policy decision making. This could be informal, through being timed to provide an output that due to its scale will impact on policy; or formalised by being endorsed by a politician from the outset.
— **Multi platform:** A wide variety of online and offline approaches is required, exploiting the potential of new technologies while supporting communities to deliberate themselves.
— **Coordinated:** The various approaches used must be grouped together under a single banner and connected through new technology.
— **High Profile:** Whatever we do must exist in the wider public consciousness.

Although the components above are central to its development, at this stage no one yet knows what a truly national public engagement process will look like. We have learnt that participatory mechanisms often develop in unforeseen ways. After all, ten years ago who would have thought Number 10 e-petitions would act as a platform for anti road-pricing? Or that *Big Brother* would have changed the face of television? Or that Facebook would be overtaking email use for most UK students?

These uncertainties reflect the pace of modern society and present a challenge to any politician or official seeking to engage the public. When facing those tough, indeed wicked, policy challenges of health and environment, a new and groundbreaking approach is needed to match the scale and complexity of the problems. To solve the problems, we need to involve people and we need to take risks in doing so. At worst there may be a few ill-conceived headlines about wasting public funds, yet at best we might actually create the conditions that enable us to make some headway on the most critical issues facing society today, and to prepare more effectively for yet more uncertainty and wicked problems arising tomorrow. Making the decision to take on that challenge would show that we really have entered the age of New Politics.

Notes

1   Fung, A. 2002. Creating deliberative publics: governance after devolution and democratic centralism. *The Good Society* 11(1). http://muse.jhu.edu/demo/good_society/v011/11.1fung.pdf

2   Dunleavy, P., Margetts, H., Bastow, S., Pearce, O. and Tinkler, J. 2006. *Why is it so hard to achieve organizational innovation in government?* EDS Innovation Research Programme. London: LSE.

3   OECD. 2001. *Citizens as partners: information, consultation and public participation in policy-making.* Paris: OECD, 23, 24, 28.

4   Wicked problems are the highly complex, circular, fluid and changeable social problems that society faces to which there is no one simple solution. See Rittel, H. and Webber, M. 1973. Dilemmas in a General Theory of Planning, *Policy Sciences* (4), Amsterdam: Elsevier Scientific Publishing, pp. 155-159.

5   Mortimore, R., Clark, J. and Pollard, N. 2007. *Blair's Britain: the political legacy*. London: Ipsos MORI.

6   Page, B. 2007. Speech at MORI Summer Review Conference. London.

7   http://www.number-10.gov.uk/output/Page13012.asp

8   http://www.conservatives.com/tile.do?def=conference.2005.news.story.page&obj_id=125411

9   http://www.number10.gov.uk/output/Page12155.asp

10 Rawnsley, A. 2003. This one man show wants to run and run. *Observer*. 28 September.

11 Citizens' juries. The events that have become known as Brown's citizens' juries are officially referred to in the UK as Citizen Summits and in the US as 21st Century Town Hall Meetings. They are not citizens' juries, which are much smaller, similar to a judicial jury.

12 Pigeon, N. 2004. *An evaluation of GM nation*. Norwich: UEA; Burgess, J. and Chilvers, J. 2004. *An evaluation of COWRM*. London: UCL; Warburton, D. 2004. *Evaluating the national waste dialogue*. London: Environment Council; AEA Technology. 2005. *An assessment of science and technology public engagement*. London: Council for Science and Technology.

13 Gavelin K., Wilson, R. and Doubleday R. 2007. *Democratic technologies?: The final report of the Nanotechnology Engagement Group*. London: Involve.

14 http://www2.aebc.gov.uk/aebc/reports/gm_nation_report_final.pdf

15 http://www.dwp.gov.uk/pensionsreform/debate/final_report.pdf

16 http://www.dh.gov.uk/en/Publicationsandstatistics/Publications/PublicationsPolicyAndGuidance/DH_4138622

17 AmericaSpeaks. 2004. *Millions of voices*. Washington: AmericaSpeaks.

18 Paxman, J. 2007. James MacTaggart Memorial Lecture, Edinburgh, 24 August. Ashley, J. 2007. Television is in crisis, and a rush to shock won't help. *Guardian*. 27 August.

19 Kohut, A. 2000. Self-censorship: counting the ways. *Columbia Journalism Review*. May/June.

Part four: Participation Nation – The Seminars

Better things to do with our time? A Conservative vision of citizenship

13 March 2007, Local Government House, Smith Square, London SW1P 3HZ

Speakers: Rt Hon Oliver Letwin MP, Bill Wiggin MP, Mary Ann Sieghart (*The Times*) Ben Page (Ipsos MORI), chair: Richard Wilson (Involve)

Ben Page opened the seminar asking "How can we make involvement work?" Page stressed that people do not feel listened to and presented the challenges to good participation. Taking local area forums as a case study, Page noted a gap between high public support for these mechanisms (82%), individual desire to be involved (26%) and actual participation levels (2%). Further, Page highlighted the strong correlation between levels of satisfaction with local councils against "feelings of influence". Furthermore, there is a strong correlation between levels of satisfaction and "opportunities for participation". Page concluded the presentation noting the tensions which could arise in a stronger public realm between a strong public and weak government, but arguing that ultimately government needs to give more responsibility back to people, or persuade them to take it.

Oliver Letwin began by advancing the view that Labour's overly "managerial approach" to the public sphere was damaging to participation. Giving the example of his own local primary care trust, Letwin maintained that focusing on management targets as set by central government was in fact hampering service delivery. Letwin advanced this position, arguing that the use of consultation in conjunction with this managerial approach limits the chances of individuals to influence the decisions that affect their lives. He elaborated further that the culture of management directs individual action towards pre-defined outcomes and therefore consulting individuals will at best change the management approach of government. Letwin argued that a culture shift was needed away from the managerial approach towards the development of frameworks used to better enable individual action but not towards pre-defined outcomes. He stressed that government must use its tools to create a framework for people to move in a socially desirable direction. Letwin concluded that "people participate when they know it makes a difference".

Mary Ann Sieghart addressed the issue of participant motivation. Sieghart discussed the extent to which time constraints may determine levels of public participation. She argued that participatory activities tend to demand large time commitments and that this could account for low take up. She iterated that if consultation is to take place it must be meaningful and be seen to be a good use of individuals' time, and went on to relate this to her personal experiences of community participation as a participant.

Bill Wiggin concurred with Letwin's criticism of "managerial government" and argued that individuals would only participate if they felt that it would make a real difference, particularly to their own lives. His key message was that a Conservative government would seek to devolve power to the public in a more effective manner than the current government, and in doing so to help address difficult issues of voter apathy. Wiggin argued that what appears to be voter apathy was actually public disillusionment with politicians. Low levels of public trust, he argued, are largely to the result of unreasonable promises being made by government politicians who then fail to deliver on them.

My space not yours? Public engagement and the YouTube generation

26 April 2007, Local Government House, Smith Square, London SW1P 3HZ

Speakers: Ros Taylor (the *Guardian*), Iain Dale (18 Doughty Street), Tom Steinberg (MySociety), Nigel Dacre (Ten Alps Digital TV), Oswin Baker (Ipsos MORI), chair: Richard Wilson (Involve)

Oswin Baker opened the seminar with a presentation discussing the implications of Web 2.0 for public policy. Baker presented the shift from Web 1.0, static content/software which could be sold, to the current trend of user-driven content which is about "participation not publishing". By profiling the users of the new user-centred online tools such as blogs and social networking sites, Baker highlighted that Web 2.0 is largely driven by young people (16–24 year olds). Baker contrasted this new type of young person with the 1950s conception of "the teenager", demonstrating, what he calls, a "quantitative change" in today's "Generation @". How, Baker asked, could policy makers harness the power of Web 2.0?

Tom Steinberg noted that in among the trends of "Generation @" highlighted by Baker there was a decline in the use of email. Steinberg questioned whether politicians should be active in young people's space and argued that civic culture could not be imposed on people but should instead evolve from the development of products and initiatives which meet people's needs. Innovation driven by demand, he claimed, may have political side effects but these side effects should not be the basis of the design.

Ros Taylor warned that the danger of the MySociety approach is that politics can become simply a matter of "getting my problem fixed". Taylor argued that "we haven't created excitement about politics". Citing the Conservative leadership contest, Taylor flagged up some exceptions which had captured the public's imagination. She noted that much of the public, particularly women, are put off by the individualistic, confrontational politics of the Commons.

Iain Dale began by arguing new media gives a voice to people who have never had one. He noted Doughty Street's own citizen journalist programme, which allowed individuals to make short films about the issues which affected them. He urged politicians to "take risks" and reach out to the public through new media, citing the blog by Nadine Dorres MP as a good example.

Nigel Dacre made the case that new media gave a voice not just to individuals but organisations, particularly small organisations. He also noted that connecting different forms of media can make a more powerful impact than using only one medium, using the example of *Teachers TV*, which began as a TV channel but the accompanying website has now become the more important medium.

A question about whether the growth in uptake of new technologies makes it difficult for individual voices to be heard was discussed at length by the panel. Dale drew on his experience of running a blog arguing that blogs filter into the mainstream media and are filtered from the "noise" by the choice of what people think are the most important issues. Taylor argued that what was picked up by the mainstream press was not always the most important. She noted that she had yet to see any blogs from midwives about NHS or hospital policy. A question about whether technology would widen or deepen participation was answered by Steinberg, who said this was the wrong question, maintaining that participation should be a natural side effect of giving people what they want. Baker argued that if the physical reality on the ground is ignored then participation initiatives will fail because new initiatives will be delivered to communities who either do not want them or have no need for them. He gave the example of a community centre delivered to a community when there was no demand identified and which was subsequently left unused.

Better things to do with our time? A progressive vision of citizenship

1 May 2007, Local Government House, Smith Square, London SW1P 3HZ

Speakers: Rt Hon Ed Miliband MP, Tim Horton (the Fabian Society), Polly Toynbee (the *Guardian*), Ben Page (Ipsos MORI), chair: Stella Creasy (Involve)

Page repeated his presentation regarding the condition of the public realm as previously given at the seminar with Oliver Letwin on the same subject. In response, Ed Miliband set out how the traditional vision of citizenship was limited because it did not take into account the expertise of the user in determining how a service was provided. A progressive view of citizenship, Miliband claimed, must start with respect for the citizen and the citizen's expertise. Above this, it must empower citizens. He explained that this is partly about choice for individuals, but also about empowerment of groups, such as young people. Furthermore, Miliband argued, beyond empowerment we need accountability. He referred to Tony Benn's five questions to those in power, which culminate in "How do we get rid of you?". Miliband acknowledged that people need to know the answers, and know who to complain to; in some services, such as the Police, it is often unclear. Finally he argued, progressive citizenship must be reflected not just in our relationships with the state, but with each other, through greater solidarity. This is crucial, as change happens not just when governments want it but when citizens demand it with pressure from below. The goal, Miliband concluded, must be an enabling state working with empowered citizens.

Polly Toynbee argued that one of the problems with New Labour was that it did not "set up a flag"; that is, they did not state their values publicly. This, Toynbee claimed, has led to a loss of the traditional tribal loyalty associated with political movements and diminishes the perception of continuity of government initiatives. Toynbee argued that by introducing the choice agenda, government had given people individualism and consumerism instead of citizenship. Re-energising the public sphere, she claimed, requires government to answer the question: "Involved in what and for what?". She concluded by re-emphasising the need for government to offer citizens something to believe in.

Tim Horton began his response noting the healthy state of single issue groups in the public realm. He tied this to the central theme of tackling anti-political sentiment which, Horton claimed, is based on a misunderstanding of the political process. Elaborating, Horton explained that anti-politics is based on an individualistic distancing from the state and the public realm. He explained that this discourse allows anti-political actors the freedom to make blanket criticisms of government while absolving themselves of any public responsibility. Horton continued by highlighting the differences between democratic decision making and consumerism and arguing that in creating consumer society politicians create unrealistic perceptions of the way in which government works. Horton noted that the Left have an interest in fighting anti-political sentiment based on the shared ideology of solidarity and collective sentiment.

Responding to questions about making participation meaningful and tailoring opportunities for young people, Miliband recognised that time constraints were a key factor in determining participation and noted that "government can consult too much". Page said growing up is about young people finding themselves, not just about understanding society, and that should be taken into account when designing participation initiatives. Toynbee argued that introducing measures such as voting at 16 and proportional representation would help overcome the current "disconnect between the expectations and realities of collective decision making".

Competing for airtime: is the future of participation corporate, social or political?

21 May 2007, Local Government House, Smith Square, London SW1P 3HZ

Speakers: Rt Hon John Denham MP, Arlo Brady (Freud Communications), Andy Martin (Cancer Research UK), Scott Keiller (Starbucks), Polly Billington (the Today programme), Simon Atkinson (Ipsos MORI), chair: Stella Creasy (Involve)

The seminar began with a presentation from Mori's Simon Atkinson, which highlighted the move from traditional forms of political participation and public disillusionment with elected officials and political institutions. Atkinson considered the high levels of participation in charitable activities and the rise of consumer activism, particularly in light of recent concern for the environment.

Scott Keiller set out Starbucks' role in revitalising the public realm through their joint programme with the Royal Society of Arts in which over 3,000 people took part in conversations hosted by Starbucks, talking about the issues that concerned them. Following questions about the representativeness of such a programme Keiller argued that Starbucks was not trying to replace more accountable forms of engagement, but instead offering new forms of participation that could reach people who currently have little interest in traditional forums.

Andy Martin from Cancer Research UK considered what lessons could be drawn from high levels of participation in charities, noting that advocacy and "individual involvement in the cause" was a key driver for participation. Introducing the idea of "self-actualised" volunteers, Martin noted their involvement is largely influenced by an awareness of political and social factors and that trust is an important feature of their relationship with the charity. However, Polly Billington argued that the public's perception of NGOs led to levels of trust which were not always justified. Martin concurred that accountability, particularly scrutiny from the media, will become much more important for charitable organisations as a result of increasing public involvement in the sector.

Arlo Brady drew on the success of his involvement with Live Earth and Make Poverty History campaigns to outline the factors he felt most important to engaging individuals. Elaborating on Andy Martin's point about public trust in charities, Brady noted that social legitimacy with the target audience was underpinned by the extent to which an organisation appeared honest and consistent. By adopting a partnership approach movements like Make Poverty History created in participants the feeling of being part of a community – Brady concluded that this was key to the campaign's success.

Polly Billington focused her discussion on the idea of political dissent, arguing that freedom to dissent has been a long celebrated British political tradition but was open to abuse in some parts of the media. However, she argued that the current appetite for consensus in participation should not preclude the freedom to disagree, stating: "Talking about the issues does not necessarily lead to rationality."

John Denham began by questioning the underlying assumptions of what "politics" is. Denham picked up on Billington's points emphasising what he called the "arbitrary division in the media between the political and non-political" which, he claimed, leads to a separation of party politics from other forms of politics. Denham argued that the "political" needed to be redefined and made relevant to citizens in order to increase public trust in formal political mechanisms. Denham argued that recent trends of voter turnout did not change the fundamental truth that "if choices are real and matter to people, they will vote".

In response to a question about the role of consumers in changing companies' behaviour Brady stated categorically that "ethical consumerism changes businesses", arguing that while business has been responsive to consumer demands, government has been much slower at responding to public trends. Denham argued that government often stimulated the development of new social trends, giving the example of the "5 portions a day" slogan, which is now used as an effective marketing tool by the private sector. Denham argued that politicians can harness ethical consumerism for policy needs such as anti-social behaviour.

The session concluded with an observation from Simon Atkinson that any participatory form must consider the limitations on individuals' time: "people are very busy".